ARCHITECTURE OF
SHAME

HO KWONCJAN

Marshall Cavendish
Editions

Published by Marshall Cavendish Editions
An imprint of Marshall Cavendish International

A member of the
Times Publishing Group

Other Marshall Cavendish Offices:
Marshall Cavendish Corporation, 99 White Plains Road, Tarrytown NY 10591-9001, USA • Marshall Cavendish International (Thailand) Co Ltd, 253 Asoke, 12th Flr, Sukhumvit 21 Road, Klongtoey Nua, Wattana, Bangkok 10110, Thailand • Marshall Cavendish (Malaysia) Sdn Bhd, Times Subang, Lot 46, Subang Hi-Tech Industrial Park, Batu Tiga, 40000 Shah Alam, Selangor Darul Ehsan, Malaysia.

Marshall Cavendish is a registered trademark of Times Publishing Limited

National Library Board Singapore Cataloguing-in-Publication Data

Name: Ho, Kwoncjan.
Title: Architecture of shame / Ho Kwoncjan.
Description: Singapore : Marshall Cavendish, [2019]
Identifier(s): OCN 1110546989 | ISBN 978-981-4841-99-3 (paperback)
Subject(s): LCSH: Singaporean fiction (English) | Architecture--Fiction. | Architecture--History.
Classification: DDC S823--dc23

Printed in Singapore

CONTENTS

DEDICATION

When anthropologist Margaret Mead did her research in Samoa, she took a short holiday at a nearby island, where cannibalism was still practiced. Needing some coffee, she entered a provision store – where she saw three glass jars, crammed with human brains.

The first jar was labelled: *Engineers' Brains, $5.00/gram.*

The second jar: *Accountants' Brains, $7.00/gram.*

But, the third one surprised her: *Architects' Brains, $1,000.00/gram.*

She asked the shopkeeper: "Why are the architects' brains *so* valuable? Is it because they are creative, imaginative and talented?"

The shopkeeper gave her a hard look. "Lady, have you any idea how many architects we have to *kill*, just to get *one lousy gram*?"

After completing her research, Ms Mead returned to the same island, and to the same provision shop. Everything was the same, or almost:

Engineers' Brains, $5.00/gram.
Accountants' Brains, $7.00/gram.
Architects' Brains, $0.50/gram.

She turned and stared at the shopkeeper. "What's going on? Why did the architects' brains become so cheap? Last time it was a thousand dollars per gram – and now it's just fifty cents!"

The shopkeeper beamed. "*Technology*, madam! We now have a new device – it just *sucks* the brains out of their ears! Five seconds flat – and they walk out whistling!"

Ms Mead was stunned. "You mean – they are still *alive?*"

The shopkeeper sighed. "Lady, *everybody* knows that architects *never* use their brains."

This book is dedicated to my fellow-architects and their microscopic brains.

PREFACE

Every year, schools of architecture around the world hatch out batches of fresh-faced architects, bright-eyed and bushy-tailed, eager to inflict their talent on the long-suffering world.

But before receiving their degrees, the graduates are herded into the school's underground dungeon. You may not believe it, but *every* school of architecture has such a secret dungeon, cold and dank, lit by flickering torches, tastefully decorated with iron shackles and skeletons. Here the trembling graduates are told the dirty secrets of our profession: the boo-boos, blunders and misdeeds of various architects down the ages, resulting in...

A hole in the middle of a roof...
A bakery that exploded...
A cathedral with mismatched towers...
A temple built ass-backward...
A tomb the corpse can't get into...

These are shameful secrets, whispered by one generation of architects to the next, but carefully kept hidden from the rest of world. And to enforce it, the Dean of the faculty then appears, masked and dressed in black like Torquemada – the Head of the Spanish Inquisition – and the graduates are forced, at sword point, to swear an Oath of Silence.

"… and if I whisper a word of this to anyone, or post it on Facebook or Instagram, may the lightning strike me; may I die a thousand deaths! May I be crucified upon my T-square, and my laptop explode on my lap; may my ACAD files turn to mush, my SketchUp files turn to ketchup, and my very cursor be cursed…"

Oh, it is a terrible oath, the equivalent of *omertà,* the Mafia code of silence. If you betray it, you will find on your pillow, not a horse's head, but your own.

Why such secrecy?

Because if the public finds out what we architects *really* do (aside from doodling endlessly) – we'll all be out on the streets, selling apples (or worse, durians) from little carts. And not only architects, but engineers, surveyors, masons and carpenters will also suffer the same fate.

Nobody will dare to build anything anymore, and we'll all end up living in caves.

But it is time the world learnt the truth. I will break this tyranny of silence, this *omertà!* In these pages I will dare to point fingers and name names, and reveal the idiotic mistakes and nefarious skullduggery practised by my profession – not to mention contractors and owners – down the ages, right up to modern times.

Dear reader, brace yourself to face the shocking truth.

01 THE *REAL* SECRET OF THE PYRAMID

Probably more nonsense had been written about the Great Pyramid of Cheops than any other building on Earth: it was built by aliens from outer space; it was an ancient astronomical observatory; it focused cosmic power and sharpened razor blades… However, the real mystery was this: for a building of such enormous size, why does it contain so little space?

Until recently, it was thought that the Great Pyramid contained only a Descending Corridor, which led to an Ascending Corridor (apparently King Cheops couldn't quite decide whether to go up or down) plus a few small chambers, today all empty. And these chambers are *small* – smaller than a squash court, which makes one wonder – where did the King store his food, clothes, jewellery, furniture and all the other luxuries he surely needed for the Afterlife?

Why build such a massive tomb with virtually no useable space inside?

In 2018, Egypt sent a top-secret team to Singapore – to learn from our Captive Merlion Breeding Programme. (If you think the Merlion is invented by the Singapore Tourism Promotion Board in a fit of phantasmagoria, learn that our genetic engineers had grafted genes from an orangutan into a dugong.)

The Egyptians wanted to know how we Singaporeans did it. They wanted to breed a Sphinx. "We tried many times," they wailed. "But it always came out looking like Donald Trump."

Of course, no government ever gave up a secret without getting one in exchange. WTO defines this as 'fair trade'. (Schoolboys do it too: *I'll show you my report card if you show me yours.*) After intense negotiation, the Egyptians agreed to let us in on *their* big secret: *The Hidden Chambers of the Pyramids.* However, to ensure silence, they would reveal it only to *architects.* (That's because architects *can't* talk. We architects just draw, or at least pretend to.)

When our little group of excited architects arrived at Cairo Airport, we were met at the gate by Fatimah, the director of Egypt's Secret Museum.

"Secret Museum?" we asked her, puzzled. "What's the point if nobody knows it's there?"

"Just wait, I'll tell you," Fatimah smiled.

We were bussed straight to Giza. I will not trouble you with yet another awestruck description of the Wonder of the World, for the Wonder of the World looked like a triangular ant-heap. The Great Pyramid was crawling with tourists – the Americans huffing their way up, Germans puffing their way down, Chinese yelling at their children, Japanese taking shots of each other…

I noticed a man surreptitiously hack a bit of stone off one of the blocks and pocketed it.

Fatimah followed my gaze. "Souvenir hunter," she said, contemptuously.

"Can't you stop them?" I asked.

"It would take an impossible number of CCTV cameras," she sighed.

I also noticed an oddity, halfway up the east side. It was a little wooden shack, erected against huge slabs of stone, and on its padlocked door was a sign: "NO ENTRY EXCEPT AUTHORISED STAFF (This is not a toilet.)."

But before I could ask, the bus stopped at the boat museum, built to house the ancient ship that ferried the pharaoh to his final resting place. The restored ship was magnificent, and we all went 'ooh' and 'aah', but Fatimah seemed curiously embarrassed, and ushered us into a little briefing room. It was here that the real surprise hit us…

"*The pyramid is full of holes!*" Fatimah told us.

Whilst we gaped at her, Fatimah continued: "There are *hundreds* of chambers hidden within it. Actually, we knew this all along – it's an extremely ancient lore, handed down by generations of architects – but nobody knew where the chambers were, until the 2016 Neutrino Survey…"

Neutrinos are tiny particles that penetrate through everything, like X-ray, and can be used to detect holes and crevices hidden within apparently solid objects. The survey revealed that implanted into the Great Pyramid are hundreds of chambers, scattered at random and undetectable from the outside. In short, the pyramid resembled a piece of Swiss cheese.

Fatimah explained, "The builders laid down layers of stone blocks, but every few layers, they left a gap between blocks, filled it with grave-goods – thrones, regalia, clothes, food, everything the King would need in the next life – and then covered it with the next layer of stone. In short, all these goodies were built *into* the pyramid from the start! They could not be stolen because there were no passages that led to them! Clever, eh?"

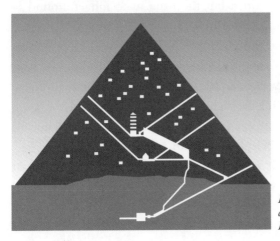

Pyramidal Swiss cheese – the Great Pyramid of Cheops.

"The grave-goods were installed even *before* the King died?" we asked. "Wouldn't they be a little stale by the time they actually buried him?"

"What's a few decades, compared to Eternity?" she replied.

"But if they were locked into solid stone, how would *the King* get to them?" someone asked.

"According to their belief, the King's spirit – his *ka* and *ba* – can travel through solid stone."

"If he had become so ethereal, why would he need all that stuff at all?"

Fatimah shrugged. "Theology is never logical… and in any case, the matter became moot. You see, the designers made one major boo-boo. They built *corridors* that led to the burial chamber. These passages were discovered by robbers long ago and the burial chamber was pillaged – including Cheops' mummy, leaving only an empty sarcophagus. So, the grave-goods remained but the King is no longer around to enjoy them. Ironic, isn't it?"

"But surely, the architects had no choice!" I protested, defending my long-dead predecessors. "They *had* to have corridors. How else would they get the King's body in?"

"They should have cremated him and poured the ashes down an air-vent," Fatimah laughed. "As you pointed out, he had become ethereal. He wouldn't need a body at all!"

"Theology is never logical," I muttered. Then, I thought of the shack I saw earlier. "Speaking of air-vents, that shack is *your* secret entrance, right?"

Fatimah nodded. "One of several. Behind the locked door is a tunnel excavated by a remotely controlled robot. It drills its way through to the chambers, and another robot goes in to retrieve the grave-goods. Thanks to the Neutrino Survey, we have a complete, three-dimensional map showing the location of each chamber. We have recovered quite a collection and would be able to open it to the public in a few years' time."

Someone said, "They would go well with that magnificent ship we just saw!"

Fatimah blushed. "Well… that ship is a fake."

We stared. Fatimah hurriedly explained, "We just copied a design left by Thor Heyerdahl. Its purpose is to hide the *real* secret – which is an underground museum built directly under it!"

"We want the real thing!" we all whined in unison. "Can we see it?"

Fatimah nodded, and pressed a button. Suddenly, nausea swept over us. We were falling! Fatimah laughed. "The entire briefing room is an elevator! We are now descending into the Secret Museum!"

Gravity returned as the descending room slowed and came to a stop. A door opened, leading to an immense underground hall. There were hundreds of glass display cases. Workers were all around, moving artefacts in, installing new exhibits…

The Secret Museum!

Fatimah led us to a glass case. "This is a throne we discovered in one of the chambers. Lovely, no?"

"Cheops must have had a big round bum," somebody giggled.

Fatimah looked pained. "Ancient Egyptians had very strong notions of proper posture. For instance, you have to sit in the exact middle of the chair. Perching casually on a corner wasn't allowed – and in this case, self-punishing!"

"Ouch!" we all laughed.

The Great Bum of Cheops.

"Why are the legs lifted up?" I asked. "The lion-claws are elevated by cylinders. Why?"

"The Nile floods annually," Fatimah said.

"You call this a flood? Having lived in Bangkok, I'm not impressed," I snorted.

On the back of the throne was a strange scene. Fatimah explained, "The female wearing the cow's horn is the goddess Hathor. And, the man is King Cheops himself."

"The goddess is holding the *ankh*, the symbol of life!" I exclaimed, proud to show off my knowledge. "It's the 'Opening of the Mouth Ceremony' and she is giving him Eternal Life!"

Fatimah coughed. "Well, that's what we *used* to think. But the inscription made it clear that she is giving him a pacifier.

King Cheops getting a pacifier.

The ancient Egyptians believed quite literally in rebirth, and when you are reborn you are just a baby."

"Why is his skirt jutting out in front?" somebody asked, curiously.

Fatimah looked embarrassed. "*Please* don't ask!"

I snorted. "It's to hide his… you know. He may be a big baby, but she is one sexy bimbo!"

Fatimah gave me a dirty look. Blushing furiously, she dragged us to another glass case. Inside were four dolls, three with animal heads and one human. She opened the case with a key and gingerly removed one of them, and with a twist unscrewed the head, revealing a hollow interior.

Ancient Egyptian thermos bottles.

"These dolls can be opened. I wonder what they once contained."

"Maybe they are canopic jars," someone murmured. "You know, to hold the mummy's heart, liver, guts and so on."

"Nah!" I scoffed. "Don't be revolting. They are thermos bottles."

In the next case was a strange, small mat made entirely of beads, but in a curved shape. "Is that a pectoral?" someone asked. "Like, you wear it around your neck, over your chest."

"No, it's a doormat," Fatimah explained.

"That's a crazy shape for a doormat," we observed.

"Not at all! You place it so the centre of the curve is at the hinge, you see, so that every time the door opened, it would sweep across the mat and clear it of debris. The mat is self-cleaning!"

"They should have reconfigured the beads to read 'Welcome'," I observed solemnly.

Self-cleaning doormat.

"Would you be surprised that they also invented the urinal?" Fatimah asked. She brought us over to the next display.

"You're joking!" we exclaimed. But here it was – King Cheops himself, in his pyjamas, standing with arms slightly raised, facing a wall. He looked a little embarrassed. "If his *ka* and *ba* are ethereal, why would he need something so – physical?"

"Don't ask," Fatimah rolled her eyes.

Ancient Egyptian urinal.

In the next case I discovered a bust of a gaunt and emaciated woman, wearing a tall blue hat of some sort. She looked like an inmate of a concentration camp. We all felt rather sorry for her.

"Who is this?" I asked.

Fatimah looked uneasy. "We are not sure. We suspect it is a prisoner of war, a captive. See how hungry and starved she looks? Poor thing, the tendons on her

Possibly a war captive.

neck are standing out. We also suspect she had been tortured – look, one of her eyes had been gouged out!"

The next exhibit was more cheerful. It was part of a food offering, but the content looked amazingly fresh, despite its millennia of storage.

"Don't be fooled!" Fatimah snorted. "It's made of painted wood."

"The King can't eat wood," I mused.

"So what? As you pointed out, his spirit is ethereal. So, they made fake food, but it contains the *spirit* of food. The

Food offering.

spirit of the King ate spirit food – right? But, come and look at what else they ate."

Fatimah led us to the next case. "Brace yourself, this may be a little shocking."

We gasped at the stone relief. "They ate *children?*"

"Frankly, we aren't sure. What were those tiny humanoids the King was munching on? They might represent children, but they might be aliens. If so, all those UFO people may be right…"

By the end of the tour, we were all exhausted. As we left the hall and went back up, Fatimah told us, "We are about half-way through extracting all these artefacts. I estimate that

The King munching on… a small creature.

within five years we would be finished and can announce it to the world, and finally open this museum to the public."

I asked Fatimah, "Why so hush-hush? Why can't you announce your findings already?"

She looked shocked. "*Of course,* we have to take all this stuff out before we announce it."

"What would happen if you announce it *now*?"

She screamed, "Haven't you *seen* all those thousands of visitors clambering all over the pyramids? Can you imagine what would happen if we tell them it is filled with treasure?"

Her voice rose to a screech. "All those tourists will *tear the pyramid to pieces.* There won't be a single stone left standing on another!"

02 **THE GREAT DITCH OF CHINA**

It had been said that the Great Wall of China is the only man-made object visible from outer space. Whether true or not, it was certainly a vast undertaking. However, it may come as a surprise to its millions of annual visitors that the Great Wall started, not as a wall at all, but as a *ditch*.

In 220 BC, King Yinzheng of Qin conquered all the other nations 'like a silkworm devours a mulberry leaf', thus bringing all of China under a single rule. He grandly named himself the First Emperor. A total control freak, he standardised the weights, currency, length of carriage axels, and most importantly, the Chinese script. (He also introduced punctuation, but that never caught on.)

Most famously, he resolved to erect a defence along the northern edge of China, to block the frequent incursions by marauding Xiongnu and other nomads.

He decided on a moat.

Since then, historians had debated his peculiar choice. One explanation was that the First Emperor followed the

School of Five Elements, and since the preceding dynasty, Zhou, was associated with fire, the new Qin dynasty must be associated with the next element, namely water. "Water extinguishes fire," the First Emperor said, despite the fact that the Zhou dynasty had already burnt out long before.

However, a more mundane reason might be that, whilst still a king, he had successfully fortified his capital with a huge moat and became convinced of its efficacy. Historian Sima Qian quoted him saying, "Nomads can't swim."

Whatever the reason, works started on a vast moat in the rugged terrain of north China. It was to be fifty metres wide and over a thousand kilometres in length. To fill it, a canal was dug from a tributary of the Yellow River to bring water to the northern hills.

It was a measure of how megalomania utterly blinded rulers to the ordinary facts of life – and how fear instilled by tyranny caused men to keep silent – that 210 kilometres of the moat was actually dug, and the canal was completed, before an engineer named Wan finally plucked up the courage to tell the First Emperor a simple fact…

Water is *flat*.

The moat, running up and down the hills, would never work. Any water introduced into it would simply flow to the lowest point and spill out. The idea couldn't hold water – no more than the ditch.

After burying Wan in the ditch, the First Emperor summoned the Grand Master of Dao, who had been busy with preparing the Elixir of Immortality. "Forget Immortality,"

The First Emperor, being told his idea wouldn't hold water.

he told the trembling Grand Master. "Make water flow uphill or you'll be mortal tomorrow!"

The Grand Master summoned his disciples, and made a grand procession to Dead Camel Pass, where the newly completed canal intercepted the moat. As the First Emperor watched, the priests burned incenses, beat drums and chanted incantations. Then, they summoned up their collective *chi*…

They were buried right next to Wan.

A group of Confucians also came, uninvited. They brought along wooden stools, drank wine, and jeered at the Dao Master and the First Emperor: "The *'Way'* that can't be spoken is a cul-de-sac!"

They were buried next to the Daoists.

By now, it was obvious that gravity would obey no one, not even an emperor. So, the Master of the Legalist School said, "Divide the moat into sections, each one higher than the next, separated by bunds to hold in the water! Thus, the Son of Heaven may impose his will upon All-Under-Heaven!" This modification was hurriedly carried out at a section of the moat, but even before they were filled with water, the First Emperor could already see how the enemies could simply walk *on* the bunds.

"I might as well put up a sign saying, 'Welcome to China'!" he growled.

The Legalists were buried in the ponds.

These mass graves were discovered in 1994. The 887 skeletons were badly decayed, but in the hand of one was a strip of bamboo, on which was hurriedly scrawled the words, "Never tell an emperor a lie."

Another bamboo strip said, "Never tell an emperor the truth."

A third strip declared, "Never tell an emperor *anything*."

The First Emperor then decided to make a virtue of necessity and proclaimed that digging the ditch was merely a clever ruse to deceive the nomads. The *real* intention was to extract soil for building a mammoth rammed earth wall, which he proceeded to encase in brick and stone. Thus, the Great Wall of China came into being, running roughly parallel to the now-abandoned ditch.

In the two millennia since, the 'Great Ditch' had eroded, and only traces of it remains. A few valleys are all that can be seen today – a silent and nearly forgotten testimony to the absurdity of absolutism.

AFTERWORD

According to Sima Qian, the First Emperor decided to bury eight thousand soldiers next to his tomb, to guard him

The valley (left) is a remnant of the 'Great Ditch'.

forever. After all, he had already buried nearly a thousand Daoists, Confucians and Legalists.

"Let a hundred flowers bloom," he proclaimed. "But only one hole be dug."

His minister Li Si whispered, "Scholars wield ink-brushes, but soldiers got *real* swords."

The First Emperor took the hint and made terracotta dummies instead.

03 **WRONGLY ASSEMBLED**

The Ise Shrines are the oldest buildings in Japan, but paradoxically, among the newest as well. Since the original construction some two thousand years ago, each was replaced by an exact duplicate every twenty years, symbolising the Shinto belief in death and renewal.

The trouble is: it's been rebuilt wrongly.

The main shrine at Ise –
wrongly built.

This tradition of rebuilding was interrupted only once. Starting from the 1460s, Japan entered into an exceptionally turbulent period, when various warlords battled incessantly for supremacy. Although the shrines were not attacked, they were neglected, and rebuilding became sporadic and eventually ceased. By 1584, Toyotomi Hideyoshi had reunified Japan, and the island was at peace at last. Hideyoshi asked his second-in-command, Tokugawa Ieyasu, to take charge of resurrecting the shrine. Visiting the site, Ieyasu found the shrine in a parlous state.

"… Everything had fallen. The outer walls were in ruins, the gates gone, the bridges collapsed. Of the Naiku (inner) Shrine, nothing remains standing. Columns, beams and floorboards have fallen and lay in a tangle, with weeds and bramble half-covering them. I judge they were not destroyed by human hands, for they bear no signs of fire nor axe, but there had been numerous typhoons and earthquakes, and these have shaken and loosened the building until they fell apart…"

Ieyasu sent a team of carpenters to rebuild the shrine. With the fanatical attention to detail typical of the Japanese, the men carefully took apart the tangled heap and replicated each individual member. It helped that no nails had been used, so the components simply fell apart cleanly, without tearing; and that many of the pieces were symmetrical, so even if one half was missing, one could deduce the whole by mirroring. After fashioning a complete set of components, the team then tried to reassemble them, like a gigantic set of Tinkertoy.

They ended up with what we see today: two main columns supporting a long ridge beam, and smaller columns on either side supporting the eaves of the roof. The whole thing stood on a raised platform.

But there were three pieces left over – two main columns and one ridge beam. After some debate, the carpenters concluded they were meant as *spare parts*. After all, they were the three most important elements, bore the greatest weight and were the most difficult to replace. So, the original builders must have made extra pieces and kept them in store. If a piece broke, it could be swiftly replaced.

Not sure where to put these spare parts, the carpenters slotted them under the platform. In every subsequent rebuilding, these extra pieces were also replicated and placed under the platform, even though they were never used. All the same, people wondered. Why *two* spare columns? Surely one would have sufficed. It was unlikely that both columns would break at the same time, so why have two spares?

That was not the only mystery surrounding the shrine; in fact, there was an even older one. In Lady Murasaki's eleventh century novel, *The Tale of Genji*, Prince Hikaru Genji paid a visit to Ise:

"… When the Prince arrived, he changed into flowing garments of the purest white, and since the sky was still clear, he rested in a pavilion, and his attendants served him fragrant tea. But soon storm clouds gathered and drops of rain fell. The Prince hurried to the shrine and entered – for who can tell how long

the rain will last? With joy in his heart he was purified; he raised his hands in gratitude, his garments clung to him, and he slowly walked down the middle of the hall… When he reached the far end, the sky suddenly cleared, as if someone had pulled back a veil, and the Sun Goddess Amaterasu smiled upon him. It was a very good sign…"

Why should Prince Genji wait *until* it rained before entering the shrine? Why did he hurry, as if fearing the rain would stop? Why did his 'flowing' garment cling to him? Nobody knew.

In 1949, Toshiro Ramen was born near Ise, and after participating at one rebuilding, he became bitten (as he put it) "by the wood bug". He trained as a carpenter, and his uncanny skill and devotion to ancient wood-carving techniques eventually won him the title of 'Living National Treasure'.

The Ise Shrine became his specialty, and he travelled all over Japan to give lectures to architectural students. For that purpose, he made himself an 'Ise Kit' containing scaled-down replica of every component of the main shrine, including the three spare parts. For the roof, he sewed two pieces of padded cloth, painted to resemble thatch. He would assemble the model in front of the students, to show how it was put together; and at the end, he would push the extra columns and beam under the platform of the completed model, as tradition dictated.

One night, he took the kit home, left it in the living room, and went to bed with a headache. The next morning, he found an odd-looking thing on the floor – his six-year-old granddaughter Sachiko had found the kit and assembled it whilst he slept. He was amused to see that she had separated the two roofs, with the two low ends facing inwards – like a butterfly roof.

He took the pieces apart and rushed to the train station. Halfway to Kobe, he suddenly realised that Sachiko had used up *all* the components – including the three spare parts. She had achieved what teams of carpenters failed to do for the last several centuries!

"It was the worse lecture I ever gave!" Ramen laughed. "I kept thinking of what Sachiko had done. When I assembled the model, I kept putting the pieces together *her* way, rather than the 'normal' way… the students probably thought I was drunk or suffering from Alzheimer's!"

Back home, he and Sachiko reassembled the kit 'her way' and studied it minutely. When he questioned her, she merely shrugged and said, "It was obvious. Four columns and two beams make two roofs, so I built two roofs!" and sauntered off to watch a cartoon.

What particularly excited Ramen was this: there were strange holes and protrusions on various pieces that served no discernible purpose, but were copied exactly, generation after generation – such was the Japanese adherence to tradition. "But assembled her way, every protrusion went into a hole. Everything fits together perfectly!"

Furthermore, this configuration explained the puzzling passage in the *Tale of Genji*. Ramen said, "The two roofs

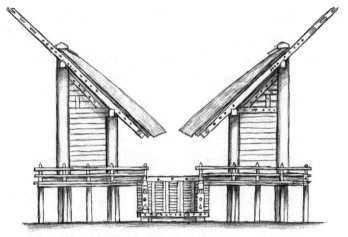

Correct form of Ise shrine, as reconstructed by six-year-old Sachiko.

were *not* meant to keep out the rain. On the contrary, they collected water and poured it down the centreline, like a waterfall. *It was a purification rite.* The Prince walked down the middle and was washed free of sin. It makes sense now! Unfortunately, the tradition was interrupted. the long period of neglect in the sixteenth century meant the correct way of assembly was forgotten. Ieyasu's carpenters made a guess, and they guessed wrong! And, we had been repeating their mistake ever since!"

Alas, the nation did not agree. When Ramen went public with this discovery, the reaction ranged from the sceptical to the hostile. The right-wing newspaper *Kamikaze* sent Ramen a plastic sword, suggesting he use a real one. Author Mishimashi predicted that the 'Living National Treasure' would soon be a dead one. Even the humour magazine

Bushido Bullshit got into the act, suggesting that Ramen was a North Korean agent sent to subvert Japanese culture.

"My life became hell," Toshiro lamented. "My lectures were cancelled. People avoided me. Even Sachiko got death threats. I wish I never, never opened my mouth!"

But unexpectedly, the people of Ise – who participated in the twenty-year cycles of rebuilding – came loyally to his defence. To the alarm of the National Diet, they declared that in the *next* cycle (2033) they would re-erect the shrine… in the 'Sachiko Way'.

A spokesman announced, "Those egg-heads in Tokyo should just shut up. Toshiro is one of us, he knows more about the shrines than anybody, and his reconstruction makes sense – we should know, *we* are the ones who dismantle the old temple and erect the new one! So next time we'll rebuild it as Toshiro had shown us…

"And if the public doesn't like it, we can always use it as a carwash."

04 A HOLE IN THE HEAD

Would you live in a house with a big hole in the roof?

And yet that is the Pantheon in Rome; for millennia, home to a multitude of gods and saints, not to mention millions of hapless tourists. How did the greatest and most impressive building of the Roman Empire end up leaking hopelessly in the middle?

The original temple was built during the reign of Augustus, by one Marcus Agrippa, known to posterity as 'Grippa the Griper'. This building burnt down in 80 AD and its replacement burnt down again, in 110 AD. (No wonder he griped.)

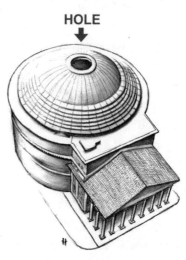

The Pantheon with its hole in the roof.

Around 126 AD, Emperor Hadrian built the present edifice, to house all the deities of Rome; a huge dome with the portico in front and a whacking big hole in middle. Oddly, Hadrian did not put his name on the portico but instead announced it as the creation of Marcus Agrippa – an action that historians ascribed to his modesty and humility.

That's what historians say. We architects know better…

When Hadrian decided to rebuild the burnt-out temple, he summoned the greatest architect of his day, Apollodorus of Damascus. But knowing architects, Hadrian wanted a second opinion, so he also summoned Horrendorus of Antioch, the most famous *engineer* of the era.

"I want a *perfect* temple," Hadrian told them.

"The perfect form is a *sphere*, of course," Apollodorus airily said. "The Greeks said so."

"How do people stand up inside a ball?" Horrendorus demanded. "A few can stand on the bottom, but everybody else will slide down and pile up in the middle!"

"A good idea if I want an orgy," Hadrian muttered. "But this is a *temple*, for Jupiter's sake."

"Flatten the bottom," Horrendorus told Apollodorus. "Every heard of a floor?"

Apollodorus glared at him. "Engineers!" he hissed. "*They flatten everything.*"

But there was no other solution – short of moving the temple to outer space and zero-gravity – so the temple ended up as a cylinder, with a hemispherical dome above it. At the

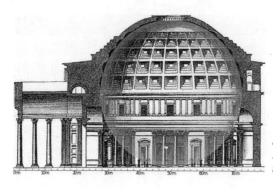

*Section across the
Pantheon, with an
inflated ego within.*

architect's insistence, however, the height had to be *exactly* the same as the width. "This way, it is *almost* perfect," he sighed. "If I inflate a perfectly round balloon in it, it will fit perfectly."

"Architects!" Horrendorus whispered to the Emperor. "Inflating their egos!"

Horrendorus had the problem of building this monster dome. Never before had anyone attempted a dome of such size. After weeks of calculations, he went to Apollodorus, who had just completed his plan for a round temple and was happily doodling little curlicues around the edges of his parchment.

"Here... I want you to thicken your walls," Horrendorus said.

"Why?"

"The dome pushes outwards and puts huge stresses on the periphery. I need heavy thick walls to act as the abutment, to prevent the bloody dome from trying to flatten itself and collapsing!"

"I thought engineers *want* to flatten everything," the architect sneered. "How thick?"

Horrendorus drew a circle around Apollodorus' plan.

"Are you mad?" Apollodorus exclaimed. "*That* thick? Are you building a temple or a fortress? This wall will be wide enough to contain several rooms!"

"Well, *put* some rooms there!" Horrendorus snapped. "You architects never provide enough storage space anyway."

Apollodorus had divided the circle into eight bays, and since one was used for the entrance, there were seven bays left, each with a plinth for a deity, and a storeroom conveniently behind – built into the thickness of the wall, just as Horrendorus proposed.

The trouble was, the Romans had over *twenty* gods and goddesses.

"We are short of accommodation," the High Priest said, glaring at Apollodorus.

"Too late," the architect shrugged. "Construction is already underway. The gods would just have to squeeze a bit!"

Jupiter was given the central plinth, facing the entrance, but he had to make room for his wife Juno. Likewise, Apollo and Diana were forced to share a plinth, being brother and sister.

"How about Venus together with Mars?" an acolyte suggested. "We all know what *they* did, right?"

The High Priest sniggered, but the Chief Vestal was scandalised and insisted they be separated.

The remaining plinths were given to Minerva, Pluto and Neptune.

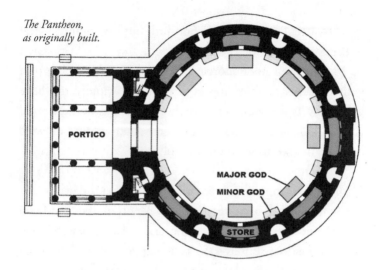

The Pantheon,
as originally built.

PORTICO

MAJOR GOD

MINOR GOD

STORE

"What about Bacchus?" another acolyte asked. "Don't we want Sacred Intoxication?"

"Maybe that's why there are two Cs in his name," Horrendorus snorted. "Drunken spelling."

Apollodorus pointed to eight small platforms placed between the plinths. "We can take eight more."

These were assigned to Bacchus, Mercury, Vulcan, Ceres, Saturn, Vesta, Maia and Plutus.

"What about Flora?" the Chief Vestal asked.

"We'll put her in the garden, with the petunias," the High Priest retorted, by now quite out of temper.

As construction rose to the base of the dome, Horrendorus erected a huge wooden scaffold, going up some forty metres to support formwork – for the dome was not built of stone, but cast in concrete.

"Architects may wax metaphorical, but we engineers deal in the concrete," Horrendorus snorted.

Meanwhile, Apollodorus decorated the lower portion with precious marbles and gold leaf, and happily ran little golden curlicues along the architrave. As the dome neared completion, the statues of the gods and goddesses were brought in and installed on their plinths.

Hadrian was impatient to see the result. When he heard that the scaffold had been removed, he went to the Pantheon unannounced, early in the morning, and ordered the watchman to open the door. But as soon as he stepped inside, he walked smack into a standing lamp, and crashed to the floor.

It was *pitch-black* inside.

His face red with fury, the Emperor screamed for the architect and the engineer, who were dragged out from their homes. "How come there's not a single window?" he yelled at the architect.

"He won't let me," Apollodorus drawled, looking at Horrendorus.

The Emperor glared at the engineer.

"Your Majesty, windows would weaken the abutment!" Horrendorus cried in horror. "We need the walls to be as strong as possible! They have to be solid!"

"Typical engineer one-track mind," the architect muttered.

The Emperor screamed, "But it's pitch-black in there! How can anyone worship in the dark?"

"We can burn a few Christians," Apollodorus mused. "But they don't give much light."

Hadrian glared at both men. "I give you a week," he screamed. "Find some way of lighting the interior, or else *somebody* will be burnt inside."

The Emperor mounted his horse and rode off, seething.

"What do we do?" Horrendorus whispered.

"I told you, cut some windows into the wall," Apollodorus suggested.

"We can't. The abutment will fail. The dome would splatter and collapse outwards."

"How about adding some flying buttresses?"

Horrendorus thought. "No. They hadn't been invented yet. Not for the next thousand years at least."

Both men were sunk in gloom.

"The stresses are worst at the base of the dome," Apollodorus mused. "But that means at the very top, there is *no* stress at all, right?"

So the workmen returned, this time with hammers, and a hole was cut into the top of the dome. As the hole widened, light returned to the interior.

"Let there be light!" Apollodorus rejoiced, looking up at the sunlight streaming in. "The eye of Heaven! Yes! That's what we'll call it – *Oculus*! It sounds better than 'a big hole', anyway."

Hadrian returned, and was pleased to see the interior illuminated. Looking up, however, he spotted the giant hole at the top. "What if it rains?"

The Oculus, cut into the dome of the Pantheon.

"The rain will fall in the middle," Apollodorus assured him. "We can still walk along the periphery."

Hadrian shrugged, and made offerings and sacrifices to each deity.

And, it started to rain.

It was not one of your well-mannered, genteel little showers, but a veritable downpour. Whipped up by the wind, the rain fell *at an angle*. The Emperor, praying before the goddess Minerva, was suddenly drenched to the skin. The party broke up in confusion as everybody scrambled along the periphery to the other side of the dome. The statue of

Minerva was left dripping wet, as though she just emerged from a bath, instead of the head of Jupiter.

"It *would* be Minerva," Apollodorus muttered. "What a wet blanket."

Hadrian, white-faced, screamed that if something wasn't done to protect the statues, somebody would get very wet… in the Tiber.

"What do we do now?" Apollodorus whispered.

"You heard him. Protect the statues," Horrendorus muttered. "What are those doors behind?"

"They are your blasted storerooms," the architect muttered. "You and your thick walls."

They looked at each other. Without a word they went to the nearest and opened the door, but shrank back at the foul smell that assailed them.

"What is that stench?" Horrendorus wailed.

Apollodorus, holding his nose, peered inside. "It's the entrails of a *sheep*… yesterday's sacrifice they hadn't yet remove. They were examining the intestines to foretell the future."

"What a stink! Why don't they read tea leaves instead?"

"Tea hasn't been invented yet. Not until the Chinese get here."

Thankfully, the next storeroom was empty. They looked around.

"If we knock down the partition, we get an alcove!" Apollodorus exclaimed.

"But such a wide opening would collapse!"

"Add some columns, then. Or how about a vault?"

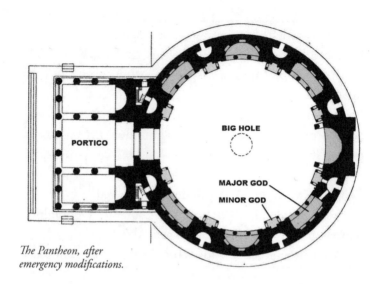

BIG HOLE

PORTICO

MAJOR GOD

MINOR GOD

The Pantheon, after
emergency modifications.

Once again workmen were called in, the storerooms were converted into alcoves, and the major gods were retracted inside. The eight minor plinths could not be retracted, so Apollodorus built little roofs above them. At least the gods were sheltered; worshippers would just have to take their chances with the weather. But there was one bonus: the retraction of the statues into alcoves freed up more useable space.

"We enlarged the space – without altering a thing!" Apollodorus and Horrendorus gleefully boasted to Hadrian, when the Emperor returned to inspect the work.

"But it still gets drenched in the middle!" Hadrian complained.

Both men shrugged. "Nobody's perfect," Apollodorus remarked.

The next day, two unidentified corpses were seen floating down the Tiber.

As for the inscription on the portico – Hadrian flatly refused to have his name placed on it.

"Marcus Agrippa started it," he grumbled. "Put his name up and let him gripe forever. I wouldn't be *caught dead* associated with this ridiculous building!"

Centuries passed. Rome fell, but the great big hole didn't.

In 609 AD, Byzantine Emperor Phocas gave the Pantheon to Pope Boniface (known to his friends as 'Bonny Face') who converted it into a church. Saints replaced the gods, not that it made much difference, for the big hole still let in rain and worshippers still had to scuttle around. A cardinal joked that the church should be renamed 'Saint Mary of the Hole' and was duly burnt at the stake. After much debate, it was given a more dignified name: Santa Maria ad Martyres. Several cartloads of martyrs' bones were excavated from catacombs and reinterred in the church – to undergo a second martyrdom, they say, given the frequent drenching.

Worshippers pray for good weather.

'The Ass' Ears'.

The poor old building had to undergo more indignities. In the seventeenth century, Pope Urban VIII (of the Barberini family) stripped and sold the millennia-old bronze ceiling within the portico. The people of Rome sneered, "What the barbarians did not, the Barberini did."

As consolation, the Pope added two little towers flanking the portico, which were instantly christened 'The Ass' Ears' by derisive locals. The Pope was undeterred. "One is for architects, the other for engineers," he said, mysteriously. "Both are asses."

05 **A TOMB TO DIE FOR**

Modern city-dwellers are resigned to spending Eternity under tiny plots of grass – or worse, inside an urn. How many of us had raised our eyes to the magnificent tombs of yesteryear, and wished that we could have a similarly grand final resting place?

The Temple of Inscription, in the Mayan city of Palenque, is one such tomb – a grand, broad pyramid with a five-door temple at the top, a secret crypt below, complete with a

A tomb to die for.

magnificent sarcophagus. Few kings had been buried with such splendour – *a tomb to die for.*

Literally.

"This is *it*?" exclaimed K'inich Janaab' Pakal, King of Palenque.

He stood on the side of a hill. Actually, he stood on a carpet of crimson cloth, spread out on the slope. Mayan kings were sacred; their feet must not touch the ground. Ever since his crowning in 615 AD, Pakal had been carried everywhere on a golden palanquin. Before he got off, the ground must be covered with scarlet cloth.

The High Priest answered, "My Lord, this is the very spot."

"The Tree of Life once grew *here*?" Pakal asked, incredulously. "I thought the Tree of Life was on a faraway island, guarded by monsters. And there's a snake that got a woman to eat the fruit..."

The High Priest snorted, "My Lord, that's just old wives' tale. According to the records, *this* is the very spot the Tree of Life once grew."

"Why here?"

"Well, it's got to grow *somewhere*," the High Priest answered, logically. "The Tree itself is long gone, of course, having given its Lifeforce to all creation... but some of its original powers still linger here..."

"Prove it!" Pakal demanded.

"Recently, an eighty-year-old man came here to pray. He was instantly rejuvenated, married a twenty-year-old bride and sired three children!"

"Wow!"

"And an elderly lady came here and became instantly pregnant!"

"Amazing!"

"In short, my Lord, if you are buried on this spot, you will become a *god* after death!"

"I'm *already* a god, didn't you know?" Pakal said, huffily. "A king is divine!"

"My Lord, you are divine only in life. After death you will enter the Underworld, like everybody else. But if you are buried here, you will become a god *forever!*"

"Very well, I will erect my tomb here. Whose land is this anyway?"

"I understand it belongs to a stubborn old man who asked for a ridiculous price," the High Priest muttered. "But no doubt he will sell to the Great Pakal…"

"Buy it from him. I don't care what it costs, I'm going to be buried right here!"

And so, the land was bought for a fabulous sum. But then, nothing is too good for the King. Of course, the fact the owner was the High Priest's second cousin was merely coincidental…

Pakal built his tomb. It consisted of a chamber with a corbelled vault and a flat roof above, containing a huge sarcophagus with a gorgeous lid. But when it came to an entrance door…

"No! My Lord, no!" the High Priest exclaimed. "No door!"

"Why not?"

"My Lord, the Lifeforce is like water. It must be *contained*

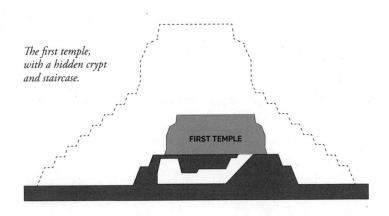

The first temple, with a hidden crypt and staircase.

within the burial chamber. If there's a door, it will spill out and be lost!"

"Then how will they get *me* in here when I'm dead?"

The High Priest thought, "Come in by the roof."

Pakal ordered a staircase to go up to the roof, but the architect pointed out that rain will get in.

"Well, build a roof above it!" Pakal snapped. This became a chamber, which he happily made into a shrine to himself. "Now, everyone can worship me!"

In 626 AD, Lord Pakal married Ix Tz'akbu Ajaw. Since he couldn't pronounce her name, he called her "Icksy" for short.

They had trouble on the very first night.

"My Lord, I was told I cannot touch you. Is that true?" Icksy asked.

"True. I'm sacred. Nobody is allowed to touch me. If you do, your soul will shrivel up and be devoured by the Jaguar monster!"

"Then how do we make babies?"

"The taboo works one way– you can't touch me, but I can touch *you*. Now lie back and stop talking!"

Alas, it wasn't much fun. Since Icksy was not allowed to hug or embrace him, or even kiss him, all she could do was to lie flat on her back, flaccid, like a corpse. For Pakal, it was not much better than necrophilia, except that Icksy wouldn't keep quiet.

"My Lord, my arms are getting cramped. May I move them?"

"Yes, just don't touch me."

They tried various positions, but it all ended in failure. Since she was not allowed to hold on to him, she kept toppling off and falling to the floor. It was ironic that the only possible position was the boring, old 'missionary style' – a millennium before the first missionaries even arrived.

Pakal had concubines, but since they were all constrained by the same taboo, he had a lousy sex life. To compensate, he started to drink heavily – but not alcohol.

Unlike most modern people, the Mayans drank their chocolate. The idea of *eating* chocolate would have seemed as strange to them as munching Coca Cola would be to us. The liquid was beaten until it became frothy, and they mixed into it all sorts of things we would consider odd – like chilli pepper. Pakal loved his chocolate, whatever it contained – indeed, he was becoming the world's first chocoholic.

"You're getting fat," Icksy informed him, sourly.

"And you are lousy in bed," he informed her.

"You crush me," Icksy said, crushingly, and went away.

In frustration, he became belligerent, conquering his neighbours, and called himself '*Pakal the Great*', which was getting literally true. To celebrate his greatness, he decided to expand his tomb.

Mayans have a clever way of enlarging their buildings. They simply added a new layer over the old structure. Pakal dismantled the small temple at the top of the temple, and added a thick layer of stone over the entire tomb – thus entombing his tomb, transforming it into a pyramid with a grand frontal staircase. At the summit, he reassembled the temple. The little internal staircase, of course, had to be extended upwards as well, to reach the higher level.

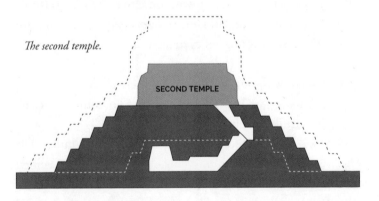

The second temple.

SECOND TEMPLE

In 663 AD, Pakal killed the lord of Pipa' and to celebrate, he enlarged his tomb once more. Once again, the internal staircase was extended upwards. At the summit, Pakal built a huge temple, with five doors.

"The one at Tikal have only one door," he gloated. "I've got five! I'm Pakal the Great!"

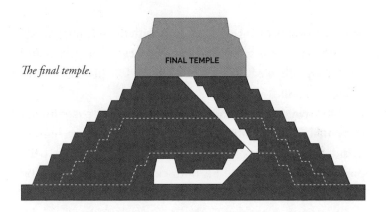

The final temple.

FINAL TEMPLE

What with easy-living and plenty of chocolate, Pakal became obese, then fat, then gargantuan. It was said that Henry VIII was so fat that three men could stand inside his trousers – well, *six* big men could huddle inside Pakal's robe. Not for nothing was he Pakal the Great…

Pakal designed his coffin. This was only a temporary receptacle, to bring him down the staircase into the burial chamber. Nobody was allowed to touch him – *even when dead* – so a coffin to carry his body in transit was a necessity. He sketched an elaborate design, and gave it to the Royal Carpenter.

The carpenter looked at the sketches. Without a word he went up the pyramid, entered the temple, and gazed at the opening in the floor, with the staircase descending down into the gloom.

"No way," he muttered. "No way can a coffin get through *that.*"

Then a hideous thought struck him. *Could he get through at all?*

The carpenter made a wooden frame, with the opening exactly the same size as the stairwell, carried it back to the palace, and stood it upright. "My Lord," he whispered. "This is the width of the staircase…"

Pakal stared at the wooden frame. He tried to pass through it frontally – impossible. Then, he tried to squeeze himself in sideways – and promptly got stuck, his enormous belly pressing on one side and his buttocks on the other. Only by sucking in his guts could he struggle free.

"We have a problem," the carpenter whispered under his breath.

"How can you let this happen?" Pakal yelled at his architect. "Why didn't you widen the staircase?"

"My Lord, the staircase was wide enough *then*."

Pakal thought back to the slim young man he once was. "I've put on weight since. When you continued the staircase upwards you should have built it wider!"

"What's the use, if the lower section is still narrow? You'd just get stuck halfway!"

The architect was used in the next human sacrifice ceremony.

Pakal summoned the Chief Mason. "Get your hammers and chisels, and widen the stairwell."

The mason blanched. "My Lord, the vault will collapse!"

The corbel vault over the staircase was made of horizontal courses of stone, each course jutting out a little over the one below, until the two sides met at the top. Cutting back the wall below meant the stone courses above would lose support – and the entire vault would collapse.

"Is there no way at all?" Pakal wailed.

"We could take apart the entire structure," the mason mused. "Right down to the burial chamber, and then rebuild everything up again, but with a wider staircase…"

"How long would that take?" Pakal asked suspiciously.

"Oh, say twenty years…"

The Chief Mason followed the architect as the *next* human sacrifice.

Pakal summoned his Councillors.

"Build another tomb," one suggested.

"No! This site is where the Tree of Life once stood. I just *got* to be buried here!"

"Go on a diet," Icksy sniggered.

Icksy was *not* sacrificed. Instead, her tongue was pierced by stingray spines.

All the same, Pakal grabbed all the diet codices he could lay hands on. He tried them all – the meat-and-potato diet, the boiled vegetables diet, the no-carbohydrates-after-midnight diet, the one that chewed each mouthful thirty-six times…

They all worked, but only up to a point, and that was when Pakal woke up in the middle of the night, stomach rumbling loudly. His retainers would scurry to bring him meat, tortillas and beans, and of course, chocolate – cups after cups of it. Binge-eating did no good – he gained back everything he lost, perhaps more.

Desperate, he called together his staff. "We can't make the staircase wider. Diet can't make me narrower. I don't have the time to dismantle and rebuild. I *can* go down that stairwell – barely – but not inside a coffin. So, when I'm dead, you must carry me down… *naked*."

The retainers were shocked. "No! No! We cannot!"

"Why not? Because you can't bear to see me indecent?" Pakal growled.

"My Lord! We cannot touch you! Not even when you are dead! Our souls will shrivel up and be eaten by the Jaguar monster! Please spare us that fate!"

"What if I command you to do so?"

"No!" the retainers cried. "We will still be struck down!"

Pakal sighed. He knew better than to force the issue. If he threatened torture, he *might* get them to promise, but what's the use? As soon as he died, all the retainers would flee, leaving his corpse to rot right where it was.

For the next month, Pakal sat in despair. He had a wonderful tomb, the best in the world, full of Lifeforce to make him eternally a god. Except, he can't get inside.

Finally, he came to a decision, the only one possible…

On the day chosen by astrologers, Pakal emerged from his palace in his palanquin and arrived at the foot of his splendid pyramid-tomb. He stepped on the crimson carpet, which stretched all the way up the grand staircase.

He looked up and sighed… *Why did I build it so tall?*

Heavily, he started to climb the steep steps. Following behind were thirty brawny young men, holding aloft a huge

'Why the hell did I build it so tall?'

sheet of white cloth. This was to catch him in case he slipped and fell, and to hide the humiliating spectacle from the crowd, since he had to crawl up the steps on all fours. His legs alone were no longer able to propel such a huge mass upwards.

It took him four hours to reach the top. He stumbled into the temple, sat down heavily on a stool, panting, sweat pouring down his face. The young men, bored out of their minds, were dismissed.

At last Pakal's heartbeat subsided. He undressed, stripping himself down to just a loincloth.

And now, the *really* hard part.

He stepped into the stairwell sideways, and slowly descended, his great belly pressing on the wall on one side, his buttocks crushed against the other. Only by sucking in his guts could he slide a few inches. Every time he inhaled, he got stuck again. Inch by inch he descended, until he arrived at the turn. Here the passage was marginally wider, and he could pause for a rest. But, not for long…

The lower section of the staircase was even worse. Although the masons had sanded down the walls, and his staff had spread lubricating oil, the constant rubbing was making his belly and buttocks very sore. But finally, he made it – with one last wriggle he plopped into the burial chamber, panting heavily, bleeding slightly and sat down on the edge of the sarcophagus. The waiting priests and acolytes prostrated themselves.

Gulping down one last cup of chocolate, he crawled into the sarcophagus, squeezing under the lid, which was propped up by wooden poles. Inside, he rotated himself onto his back. A kneeling servant offered a tray. He took from it the ceremonial bracelets and put them on. Finally, he grasped the mask – a wonderful object made of jade – and placed it on his chest.

He took one last look around. This was his wonderful tomb, the seat of the Tree of Life. Already he could feel its Lifeforce seeping into him…

Jade mask.

Eternal life! Eternal godhood! A wonderful tomb.
A tomb to die for!
He put on his mask and gestured to the priests.
"Okay. Kill me."

06 **TOO MANY DOMES**

If buildings have personalities, one can say there was never a building as sullen, obstinate and intractable as the Church of Saint Theodora, later known as the 'Mosque of Too Many Domes'. It obeyed no one, not even God; it was hardly ever useable; it confounded all human expectations. It was, in short, a building with *attitude*.

In 718 AD, Byzantine Emperor Leo III ordered his architect, Dimitri Popolopaupos, to erect a church on the summit of a hill, near the Theodosian Walls at the western edge of Constantinople. It was to be dedicated to Saint Theodora, with the usual ancillary facilities, including a monastery.

The 'Mosque of Too Many Domes' sketched by an unknown artist, circa 1860.

Popolopaupos' design was conventional: a central dome, supported by pendentives on four main arches, with semi-circular exedras on three sides and a rectangular narthex as entrance foyer. On the inside of the central dome was installed a fine mosaic, showing Christ Triumphant, and over the altar was hung an icon of the Virgin. It was dedicated in 721 AD.

A year later, cracks started to appear on the dome. The architect sheepishly admitted that the buttresses were insufficient to resist the outward thrust of the dome, and so he extended them, providing more dead weight. The cracked mosaic was patched up, but soon fresh cracks appeared, including two big ones running across the dome and intersecting near the centre. Leo III was furious, and a terrified Popolopaupos extended the buttresses once again. They stuck out so far beyond the original church, the monks decided to cover the spaces in between and turn them into useable rooms. Within the church, the mosaics were again repaired.

But meanwhile, another fissure was opening up: *Iconoclasm.*

The early church forbade 'graven images', but as Christianity spread, this taboo eroded and icons (sacred images) became ever more popular, to the point that theologians became alarmed at the way ignorant masses were worshipping the icons themselves. Leo III was also disturbed and started to regret the mosaics he had allowed in the Saint Theodora. But it was the monks there that precipitated the crisis.

The church was not popular, due to its tendency to shower worshippers with bits of plaster and mosaic. To attract devotees, the monks proclaimed that *their* icon of the

Virgin was more 'powerful' than any other in the city. For Leo III, this was the last straw. To say that *this* picture of the Virgin was more powerful than *that* one, was to imply the power resided in the picture, and not in the invisible divinity – in short, it was idol-worship. And, to think that *this* was happening in *his* church! Intolerable!

In 726 AD, Leo III rode in state to the church and gave a fiery sermon on its front steps, renouncing the 'heresy of icons'. A crash was heard within the church. Rushing inside, the mob discovered that the mosaic at the centre of the dome – at the crossing of the fissures – had fallen away, leaving Christ without a nose. Leo III cried, "Can it be doubted that God Himself does not approve of His depiction?" Spurred by his words, the mob rushed to the altar, shredded the icon of the Virgin and hacked the saints off the walls. Ten monks protested, were imprisoned and had their tongues removed.

Emboldened, Leo III ordered an attack on the biggest icon in Constantinople – that of Christ at Chalke, over the palace gate. But the ordinary people were horrified. They loved their icons and were convinced that the Emperor had become a heretic, or worse, the Antichrist. In the riot that ensued, many were killed. This was the start of a highly divisive struggle between iconoclast (icon-smashers) and iconodules (icon-lovers) that lasted a century, resulting in the death of thousands and divided the Empire just at the time it needed unity most.

In the meantime, the interior of Saint Theodora was stripped bare, re-plastered and whitewashed. Leo III announced that the previous cracks were warnings from God against idolatry, but now that the church had been purified, all would be well.

Three months later, the same old cracks reappeared.

When Popolopaupos proposed adding *another* layer of abutments, Leo III exploded in rage and ordered his arrest. Ironically, the next architect recommended precisely the same thing. Leo III had no choice. He was now committed to iconoclasm, and it was vital he kept Saint Theodora as a showcase. Thus, more buildings were added – storerooms, dormitories and refectories, although most of the monks had already fled.

The complex had grown into an untidy clutter of walls, domes, abutments and turrets, covering the top of the hill and flowing halfway down. The locals called it the 'Church of Too Many Domes'. Just finding one's way to the entrance of the church meant negotiating a maze-like warren of halls and passages. Unfortunately, the building remained unruly – not that it was ever ruly – and cracks continued to appear; and in 742 AD, after Leo III's death, the complex was shut down and left deserted.

Meanwhile, the religious struggle raged. In 797 AD, Empress Irene murdered her son Constantine VI, seized power and restored the icons. In 801 AD, she commanded Saint Theodora be covered with new mosaics. By now the church had serious fissures running every which way, but Irene proclaimed that the cracks were a sign of God's displeasure at the *loss* of the icons. (Observe how two theologies, proceeding from the same facts, could arrive at opposite conclusions; as

Voltaire remarked: "It is easy to know what God wants – you just put words in His mouth.")

In 802 AD, the refurbished Saint Theodora was reopened to an admiring public, who were especially impressed with the new mosaics inside the dome, depicting the Holy Virgin, standing triumphantly over fallen heretics (the iconoclasts). The atmosphere was festive. But scarcely had the solemn ceremony started a loud crack was heard, followed by a shower of debris.

The old trouble spot – at the centre of the dome – struck again. A gaping hole now appeared where the two fissures crossed, in the mid-point of the standing Virgin. The congregation stared, speechless. An awed worshipper exclaimed, 'Behold the Virgin birth!"

Three months later, Empress Irene was deposed.

The new Emperor, Nicephorus I, was wiser – he left Saint Theodora alone. The mosaics were removed, and the church was closed again. It had become obvious that this grumpy building had a bad-ass attitude. It hated architects, obeyed neither icon-smashers nor icon-lovers, and would cooperate with neither man nor God; an intractable and bad-tempered old harridan, best left to herself.

The real problem was not theology, but laid deeper, within the foundation itself. The hill was made of an unusual type of decayed granite, known to geologists as *schlumgh*. (Pronounced 'shlump' but with a gargle at the end.) This was formed when granite was heated to a very high temperature near a volcanic vent, and then rapidly cooled;

the thermal shock produced myriads of microscopic cracks running throughout the material. It looked like ordinary granite, and behaved as such under moderate loads, but under heavy loads the tiny fissures gave way, resulting in slow deformation and downhill creep, like molasses. The erection of more abutments was in fact worse than useless, since the additional weight increased the deformation. In short, attempts to solve the problem worsened it.

But now, left alone, the structure slowly stabilised, and remained quiet for several centuries. It survived the Sack of Constantinople by the Fourth Crusade (1204) and even the fall of Constantinople to the Ottoman Turks (1453), possibly because looters got lost inside and never came out.

The day after the conquest Sultan Mehmed II entered the city, now renamed Istanbul. He rode in state to the Hagia Sophia, where he humbly scattered earth on his turban; giving thanks to Allah, he turned his eyes up to the heavens. Later, when he rode past the vast, untidy clutter that was Saint Theodora, he *rolled* his eyes to heaven. An attendant heard him mutter "architects!" with a particularly venomous hiss.

Mehmed II was generous to his defeated foes. He summoned the Greek Orthodox Patriarch and offered him Saint Theodora as his headquarters. The Patriarch threatened suicide. Puzzled, the Sultan gave him another church instead and converted Saint Theodora into a mosque. It was renamed Camii Huma Halun, after his mother. (It seemed he didn't like her very much.) But soon, the locals were calling it the 'Mosque of Too Many Domes'.

Once again, the interior was re-plastered and repainted. A mihrab was cut into the apse – unavoidably off-axis, since the church was not built facing Mecca. But so long as no new load was added, all was quiet – until the reign of Suleiman the Magnificent (Suleiman I). The Sultan noticed that the mosque had no minaret and told his architect Sinan to "add four minarets, arranged symmetrically around the central dome". According to one legend, Sinan muttered under his breath, "Your Sublime Majesty must be joking."

Suleiman the Magnificent with his magnificent dome.

Sinan's dismay was understandable, since the entire hilltop was completely encased by buildings, domes upon domes. There was hardly an inch of bare ground left. He sent his surveyor to map the place, but after making a partial sketch, the man disappeared. "We have sent a search party and hope to find poor Hassan soon, and give him a decent burial," Sinan wrote gloomily. Hassan was never seen again, but eventually Sinan erected a single very small, very thin minaret on a buttress, and Suleiman I had to be content with that.

Unfortunately, the added weight of even a small minaret kick-started the old troubles again. In the previous centuries, the decayed building and the decayed granite had arrived at a delicate balance, but now the *schlumgh* started to deform once more. Converted buildings never function perfectly, but this one was more recalcitrant than most, and fresh cracks appeared all over the place, showering the faithful with bits of plaster and dust. Ironically, this meant the new minaret served little purpose. The devout avoided this mosque, and the muezzin suffered depression since *his* calls to prayer rarely resulted in anyone showing up.

By the reign of Selim II (Selim the Sot) the cracks became alarming – the ancient fissures across the central dome were now joined by three new ones. The Sultan's solution was unconventional: he asked the Grand Mufti to issue a *fatwa* against this 'malevolent monster'. When the Grand Mufti objected that one cannot issue a *fatwa* against an inanimate object, Selim II growled, "It swallowed a man!" and burped.

The Grand Mufti gave him a long lecture on the dangers of wine, but received a drunken snore instead, and gave up.

The worried Grand Vizier Sokollu consulted with his architect and decided on the 'tried and true solution', which was… adding yet *another* layer of buildings, not only as further abutment, but as housing for the Janissaries. Of course, this merely worsened the situation, and by the time of Murad IV, the entire complex

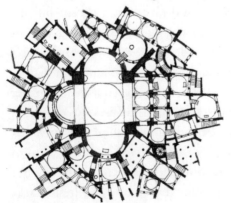

Incomplete plan by Hassan, before he vanished forever.

– which now extended right down to the foot of the hill –
looked ready to topple.

Murad IV was a bloodthirsty killer who terrorised Istanbul,
but strangely, he did the most enlightened thing possible
for the mosque – he left it alone. Perhaps he was too busy
killing people to care, although at one point (according to an
admiring Evliya Chelebi), Murad IV did propose shackling
his enemies around the base of the hill and waiting for the
avalanche to bury them. He would have been disappointed;
left alone once more, the building slowly reached a second
precarious balance with its wretched foundation. In any case,
the mosque outlasted Murad IV, who drank himself to death
in 1640, at the ripe old age of twenty-eight.

By the nineteenth century, when European tourists started
to trickle in, the mosque was once again stable, although
disused, shabby and decrepit. It was an eyesore; one Sultana
Valide complained, "It's like a horrible old relative who won't
go away and refuses to die." Yet no one dared touch it, lest the
'Mosque of Too Many Domes' collapsed completely.

Just how many domes *were* there? None of the locals could
agree, and neither could the visitors. Lord Byron, spending
a secret holiday in Istanbul, reported 516 domes; Anatole
France counted 438. Ferdinand de Lesseps, en route to the
Suez, found a whopping 1,045 domes. A local belief arose
that the true number would never be found, since it would
change each time someone counted. It was a sign that the
ultimate truth was for God alone. A more prosaic explanation
was that the complex had domes of varying sizes, many half-
domes and partial domes built to cover irregular spaces, plus

domical vaults visible only from the inside. The counts varied, therefore, according to each individual's definition of 'dome'. The only agreement, it seemed, was that there were altogether too many of them.

Having survived the fall of the Byzantine Empire, the ancient monster survived the collapse of the Ottoman Empire as well. In 1923, Mustafa Kemal Atatürk overthrew the last sultan and founded the Turkish Republic. In line with his vision of a modern, secular state, Atatürk converted the ancient Hagia Sophia into a museum, neither Christian nor Islamic.

His staff asked him what he intended to do with the 'Mosque of Too Many Domes'. Atatürk replied, "Why do you think I'm moving to Ankara?"

Wise decision. In 1925, a mild earthquake shook Istanbul. Although it was a minor temblor, the aged and crumbling structure finally lost its millennia-long struggle with gravity, and the entire complex avalanched downhill, flattening several neighbourhoods, killing forty-three people, and leaving the top of the hill as bald as an egg. It looked like Murad IV got his wish after all.

Since then, a modern apartment complex had been erected on the hill. The engineers drilled piles seventy metres down, past the *schlumgh* into solid bedrock below. And – as if in denial of its unsavoury past – the design was aggressively modern and contained not a single dome.

07 HAA-MMM-UM

In 762 AD, Al-Mansur Abbasid, Caliph of the Islamic world, started to build a new capital, Baghdad. Vast numbers of workers throughout the Abbasid Empire were brought in to construct city walls, palaces, mosques – and of course, a huge army garrison.

Napoleon Bonaparte once said that "an army marches on its stomach" and feeding a multitude of soldiers was no easy task. The camp kitchen was enormous, but although its fifty bread ovens worked day and night, supply barely kept up with demand. Furthermore, these small ovens were inefficient; they tended to lose heat, thus needing a great deal of firewood to keep going.

A year later, the Camp Commandant heard that an efficient 'super-oven' was just invented in Aleppo. He wrote to its governor, and in due course received a roll of drawings, along with detailed specifications. He handed them to the Quartermaster.

The design was simple. The firepit was a square chamber, set into the ground, accessed by a flight of steps. At its foot

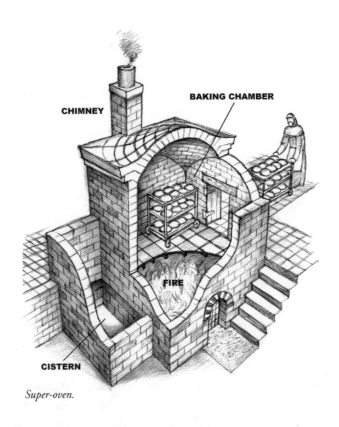

Super-oven.

was a small opening where charcoal could be pushed into the firepit, and an iron grille allowed air to enter. Exhaust exited via a chimney nearby.

The baking chamber was above the firepit, and could hold eight brass trollies, each carrying three trays of bread; thus, a great many loaves could be baked at the same time. The door was small, to limit heat loss, just big enough to admit a trolley, and was fitted with a heavy wooden double-door, kept closed by a sliding bolt. The roof was a simple domical vault.

What was innovative was the floor of the baking room. It was made of steel plates set upon steel joists, mounted above the firepit. The plates were soldered to the joists and made airtight. Metal being a good conductor, this floor would allow heat to be transmitted to the baking room, whilst blocking cinders, smoke and soot.

The Quartermaster found a site near the kitchen, and at the request of the Head Cook he added a cistern to the design, to store water. Short of space, he set it abutting the oven. This apparently minor addition was to have a major impact on history…

The Quartermaster then looked for a builder. Unfortunately, the palace was being expanded and the Caliph's many retainers also needed accommodation, which resulted in a serious shortage of builders. After a long and fruitless search, the Quartermaster glumly went to see the Camp Commandant.

"There's nobody available," he announced.

"Surely there must be one or two?" the Camp Commandant asked.

"None. Unless you count the '*Three Scoundrels*'."

"May Allah protect us," the Camp Commandant rolled his eyes.

The Three Scoundrels were so old, nobody could recall their real names; they were known as Achy, Breaky, and Harr. Achy was rheumatic, always walking bent over because his joints ached. Breaky had bad skin, breaking off in patches, he looked like an old wall with half the tiles fallen off. As for Harr, he was asthmatic, his breath coming in little wheezes; hence his nickname.

Achy, Breaky, Harr.

Should this portrayal arouse pity in the tender hearts of my readers, I advise that such sympathy is misplaced. They were the most crooked builders in the world. They were so cheapskate, they could cut corners off a circle; so devious, they could walk down a spiral staircase without turning; and so corrupt, they could enter a cemetery and send all the corpses fleeing. Conventional wisdom holds that elderly men become wise and venerable, but wisdom never had a chance to catch up with *these* three.

Not surprisingly, they had little work, were constantly sued in court, managed to survive only by accepting work from those too poor to afford a better builder, and by scrounging.

"May Allah keep us from those three!" the Camp Commandant said, again. "Is there really no one else?"

"Nobody," the Quartermaster glumly observed. "All the reputable builders are busy on the palace or building private mansions. The earliest to be free is Masood – and *he* won't be available until Ramadan!"

"What choices have we?" the Camp Commandant gloomily observed. "We need the new oven badly."

The Quartermaster shrugged. "Well, Sir, it's only an oven. What can go wrong?"

As it happened, *a lot.*

The Three Scoundrels were obsequiously grateful, bowed and kissed the floor, and promised the Camp Commandant they would use the very best materials and employ workmanship of the highest standard.

That's what contractors always said.

Of course, as soon as they got home, they threw away the specifications. "Who needs them?" Achy snorted. "We're experienced builders. We don't need to be told!"

They called in their workmen – the few they had left – and started work. Of course, being crooks, they immediately started to cut corners…

The specifications called for thick walls built of dense, heavy-duty bricks that had been fired at high temperatures, thus heat-resistant. It was essential that the oven lose as little heat as possible, so the heat within could build up to the searing temperatures needed to bake bread. They substituted sun-dried mud bricks that had never been fired at all, adding dark clay to make them resemble the real thing.

The metal floor should have been made of high-quality steel, with carefully controlled amounts of carbon – as used for fine Damascus swords. The specifications also called for careful soldering, to ensure the steel plates joined to each other and formed an airtight surface. The Three Scoundrels went to a down-and-out blacksmith and got him to make the stuff out of pig iron, heavy with dross and very brittle. As for soldering, just a few hasty blobs.

Their corner-cutting extended even to the double-doors of the baking room. Instead of an iron sliding bolt, they substituted a crappy one of old brass. How cheap could you get?

The new super-oven was completed, and the Head Baker was delighted. He shut down all the other ovens and inaugurated the new one by baking its very first batch of bread for the whole camp.

What he got was a riot. The bread that came out was damp and cold, and had barely risen. It was like eating half-cooked dough, and the soldiers threatened to burn down the kitchen. All the old ovens had to be hastily fired up again to bake a new batch – to avoid mutiny.

The Head Baker complained to the Camp Commandant, who called in the Three Scoundrels.

"Not our fault!" they cried, in unison. "The flour must have been stale!"

The grain-merchant was summoned. "My flour is of the very best quality!" he angrily insisted. "Straight from the fertile soils of Egypt, shipped to Baghdad at vast expense!"

He glared at the baker, "You must have used too much water!"

"Rubbish!" yelled the Head Baker. He glared at the Three Scoundrels, "The oven isn't hot enough!"

"The oven is plenty hot!" Achy cried. "You are blaming us to hide your incompetence!"

As anyone who has ever attended arbitration could attest, everybody was pointing fingers at everybody else. Fed up, the Camp Commandant went to inspect the new super-oven himself. He ordered it fired up again, but when the fire was roaring, he could see little puffs of smoke curling out of the cracks on the walls. Without touching the oven, he could feel the warmth – the oven was losing heat to the outside. And when he cautiously extended his hand into the baking chamber, it felt warm but hardly hot.

"Your damn oven is leaking heat!" he snarled at the Three Scoundrels.

"This cannot be. We used the best material!" Achy asserted.

"The baker is incompetent!" Breaky cried.

"And the flour is bad!" Harr wheezed.

Painfully, Achy crouched down at the small door, stuck his hand through and pulled it back hurriedly, as if scorched. "Ow! It is searing!"

"It is a furnace!" Breaky yelled.

"It is as hot as Hell itself!" Harr wheezed.

"The hell it is!" the Camp Commandant screamed, losing his temper. With one kick at Achy's buttocks, he catapulted the old man inside. Then he grabbed Breaky and Harr by the scruff of their necks and threw them inside as well, slamming the double-door shut and sliding the bolt home.

"Let us out!" Achy screamed, hammering at the door.

"Don't kill us!" Pleaded Breaky, frantic.

"We confess! We confess!" Harr yelled, panicking and wheezing.

Outside, the Camp Commandant stood, arms folded. "Hey man, hot enough for you?" he mocked.

"Sir?" the Quartermaster cautiously asked. "Granted it's

not hot enough to bake bread, but it is still plenty hot by human standards. What if they die?"

The Camp Commandant snorted, "Bah! I just want to teach them a lesson, that's all. In a few minutes I'll let them out, don't worry!"

But then something went wrong, terribly wrong. And the cause of it, ironically, was the corner-cuttings done by the Three Scoundrels themselves...

Abutting the oven was the cistern, filled with water. The previous heating and cooling had damaged the crumbly wall. With the heat applied once more, the cheap, crappy brick gave up entirely. They shattered, and water burst into the firepit, extinguishing the flames but instantly flashing into steam.

When water turns into steam, it expands spectacularly. That is why boiler-room explosions are so violent. Some of the steam escaped through the flue, but the rest pressed up against the metal floor.

The cheap, crappy floor buckled, and some of the metal plates popped off. Instantly, geysers of scalding hot steam shot up into the baking chamber, sending the temperature and humidity soaring. Under sudden high pressure, the double-doors of the chamber bulged outwards, bending the cheap, crappy sliding bolt into a shallow V-shape.

The Camp Commandant knew that something was wrong when the entire oven shook violently, and the three men inside *stopped* screaming. Instead of black smoke emerging from the chimney, white steam shot up into the air. Aghast, the Quartermaster tried to open the door, but found it jammed. The bent bolt simply wouldn't slide.

"Get an axe!" the Camp Commandant yelled. "Hurry!"

The Executioner came running, brandishing his axe. "Who is the traitor?" he asked happily. He looked at the Quartermaster.

"Not him!" the Camp Commandant cried. "The door!"

"The door is a traitor?" the Executioner asked, puzzled.

"Never mind! Just smash it down!"

With three strokes, the brawny Executioner broke open the door. Instantly a cloud of steam poured out, forcing everyone to retreat. As soon as it cleared, they rushed inside.

But it was too late. The three old men laid on the floor, inert but twisted in agonised postures.

"May Allah forgive me," the Camp Commandant whispered, ashen-faced, as they dragged the three corpses out. "May Allah know that I meant no harm, it's a terrible accident…" he wept.

Then one of the corpses stirred and stretched. "Haaah…" it said.

The next one mumbled, "Mmm…"

The third one gulped, "Um…!"

The Camp Commandant was thunder-struck. "What did they say?" he demanded of the Quartermaster.

"I think they said 'haa-mmm-um'… whatever that is."

"Hammam? What kind of word is that?"

Groggily, Achy got up and crawled over to a stool. He looked dazed.

"Are you alright?" the Camp Commandant asked him, anxiously.

"Am I alright?" Achy said, wonderingly. "I feel great!" He jumped up; his rheumatism gone. He stretched his limbs and hopped around. "I feel just great!"

Breaky sat up, his face covered with damp, drooping skin. He grabbed a towel and scrubbed his face vigorously. Dead skin rolled off in big swatches, revealing fresh new skin underneath. "Wow! I feel so fresh!" he exclaimed. He caressed his face with his hand. "I've been exfoliated!"

Achy nudged Harr. "And how about you?"

Harr sat on the floor, a look of wonder on his face. "I'm actually *breathing*," a big smile broke over his face. "I'm not wheezing anymore! The steam had cleared my lungs!"

"Hey! Hoi!" Achy pranced around, wriggling like a rock star. "Oh! My Achy Breaky Harr!"

The Camp Commandant and Quartermaster stared at each other…

After they tried the oven – cautiously – they realised that a wonderful device had just entered the world. They dubbed it 'Hammam'. The Camp Commandant persuaded the Caliph to try it. The Caliph, delighted, immediately ordered three for his palace – for men, women and one all to himself. And this was how the most civilised form of cleansing came into existence.

"What should I do with you?" the Camp Commandant scowled at the Three Scoundrels.

"Gold would be nice," suggested Achy.

"We'll settle for silver," Breaky said.

"Or how about an emerald or two?" Harr purred.

The Camp Commandant kicked their butts and sent them forth to build more hammams, all over the city, for such a discovery should be enjoyed by all. The Three Scoundrels now found themselves in great demand. They spent the rest of their lives building increasingly luxurious hammams, complete with marbled disrobing rooms, tiled hot and cold pools, massage beds and scrubs…

They became immensely rich and lived to a ripe old age.

This book contains many woeful tales of hapless architects who tried their best, but got insulted, beaten up, tortured or killed. Therefore, it was ironic how three utterly corrupt and unscrupulous cheapskates enjoyed the most spectacular and undeserved success.

Young architects take note: forget architecture, become contractors instead.

08 **BORROWED BUDDHA**

Java is the most fertile and populous island in Indonesia, and historically, the most sophisticated and advanced. It is home, not only to the capital Jakarta, but also to two magnificent monuments: Borobudur, the world's largest Buddhist monument, and Prambanan, a stately Hindu temple nearby.

Although most Indonesians today are Muslims, Borobudur and Prambanan were constructed before the arrival of Islam – when Java was ruled by the Sailendra dynasty and the Javanese followed a mixture of Hinduism, Buddhism and Animism.

Borobudur was begun around 800 AD, completely covering a natural hill, and is divided into three zones:
- *Kamadhatu* (World of Desire) – the base;
- *Rupadhatu* (World of Form) – the mid-zone, comprising of several zig-zag terraces, carved with the Jataka Tales which depicted the former lives of Buddha; and
- *Arupadhatu* (World of No-Form) – three circular terraces, adorned with seventy-two small stupas (each containing a Buddha statue) leading to a large central stupa on the summit.

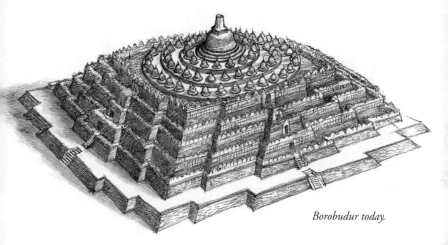

Borobudur today.

By contrast, Prambanan, a Hindu temple, was built on a flat plain, and comprised of –

- A tall central shrine devoted to Shiva, the god of Destruction, and flanked by two smaller shrines, for Brahma (the god of Creation) and Vishnu (the god of Preservation);
- Facing them, three small shrines, devoted to the conveyance of each god: Garuda, Nandi and Hamsa respectively; and
- Surrounding them, a vast array of small towers, in various states of completion.

However, by around 930 AD the court had moved, possibly because eruptions of Mount Merapi made life in the region a little dicey. Both monuments fell into disrepair. Prambanan tumbled, and the stone terraces of Borobudur bulged outwards, whilst its summit slumped unevenly; the three circular terraces started to look like warped pancakes. In

Prambanan, Hindu temple on the plains near Borobudur.

1811, Sir Stamford Raffles attempted some restoration, gave up and founded Singapore instead. "I hate jigsaw puzzles anyway," he allegedly said.

In modern times, however, both monuments were completely restored. Prambanan was re-erected, and Borobudur was taken apart, stone by stone, with a new reinforced concrete foundation built underneath and the stonework painstakingly reassembled. Today, both are UNESCO World Heritage Sites, and are amongst the most famous and most-visited places in Indonesia.

And yet, not a single visitor is aware of a dirty little secret, which the Javanese are desperately hiding from the rest of the world…

Borobudur and Prambanan were, originally, *a single building*.

Simulation of Borobudur – as it was originally.

In 800 AD, King Samaratungga decided to build a huge temple devoted to Shiva, to outshine his rivals in Angkor. "Those little Khmer kings think they're so hot, just because they built a few runty little temples!" he fumed. "I'll show them!"

His architect, Gunadharma, was Nepalese, and homesick for mountains, he situated the temple on the summit of a hill. It consisted of a central tower, representing Mount Meru, with four corner towers. The slope of the hill was terraced, in the endless zigzag pattern so beloved by Hindu architecture.

The temple was nearing completion when the King noticed a corner tower was slightly askew. Gunadharma took the tower apart and reassembled it. Then the King noticed *another* tower tilting, and the terraces below it bulging. It became obvious the problem was in the hill itself. Everyone assumed the hill was stable, but with so much weight imposed upon it, the soil started to compact; the sides bulged outwards whilst the top slumped.

Terrified, Gunadharma tried bluster. "Your Majesty, Lord Shiva is the God of Destruction – so isn't it appropriate that his temple should destroy itself?"

The King snapped, "Would *you* like to do the same, or should I do it to you?"

With all the towers tilting, Gunadharma had no choice but to take them apart and remove them from the hilltop. The King, rather deflated, chose a totally flat site some distance away, near a village called Para Brahman. He re-erected the central tower, still devoted to Shiva, but of the four corner towers, he re-erected two as shrines to Brahma and Vishnu respectively. "Maybe they felt a little left out," he thought. "Better honour them this time."

That left him with two towers, in a disassembled state. He commanded Gunadharma to reassemble them as *three* small shrines, to be erected in front of the three gods. When Gunadharma objected, the King snarled, "Two big cups of wine can surely make three small cups. What's your problem?"

After ten months of frantic juggling, Gunadharma managed the feat, similar to taking apart two Lego dinosaurs and reassembling them as three Lego rabbits. (He had to cheat a little and order a few new bits to be made.) The new complex was completed, but Gunadharma was so exhausted he retired to a Buddhist monastery, renouncing the world forever.

But what to do with the old site, with several levels of terraces leading up to a big empty space? The King summoned his councillors, but they were not much help –

"A sepak takraw field?" one suggested.

"How about a market?" another proposed.

"A football field?"

"I know! A gamelan full-moon party!"

In the end, the King decided to pass the buck.

"Honeybuns, I have the perfect birthday present for you," he crooned to his daughter, Princess Pramodhawardhani. "You have just converted to Buddhism, right? Take that terraced hill and make it into a monument for Lord Buddha!"

The Princess (who had been hoping for a ruby necklace) summoned her teacher, Bodhidharma. "What can you do with this? How about putting your monastery on top?"

Bodhidharma was taken aback. "Your Highness, Lord Buddha taught us to live humbly. How could we live on top of something so grand?" (Privately he thought: *who wants to climb down five storeys every day to collect food and climb back up again?*)

"Well, think of something!" the Princess urged. "I heard that the architect – what's his name, Goon-a-dharma or something – had just joined your order. I'm sure he would have a few bright ideas!"

Bodhidharma discussed this matter with his disciples during lunch. The food was mediocre, as expected. Buddhist monks embraced poverty, owned nothing but the clothes they wore, and begging-bowls with which they collected whatever food the local villagers could spare. Since the villagers were poor, what the monks got was apt to be a mishmash of odds and ends. Beggars couldn't be choosers, and monks shouldn't be choosy; food was for sustenance, not enjoyment. Silence was normally kept during the meal, but this matter was urgent, and Bodhidharma wanted advice – especially from Gunadharma.

"You built it," he said to Gunadharma. "Well, what do you want to do with it?"

Gunadharma whimpered. "Master, I joined monkhood just to *get away* from that blasted thing!"

"Tough. It looks like your Karma had just zinged around and come back to nail you!"

There was a silence, whilst everyone munched and looked at Gunadharma.

Gunadharma suggested, "Master, since we got those terraces anyway, let's put some carvings on them. The lowest level can represent *Kamadhatu*, the World of Desire. Then, the next few terraces can represent *Rupadhatu*, the World of Form, and we show the Jataka Tales, to instruct the devotees."

"In that case the top should represent *Arupadhatu,* the World of No-Form," Bodhidharma mused. "What do we put *there*?"

Gunadharma replied: "*NOTHING.*"

Everybody stopped munching and stared.

Gunadharma explained, "*Arupadhatu* is Formless, so we build nothing. And since the subsidence started because we put too much weight, what can possibly weigh less than nothingness?"

Bodhidharma goggled at him. "You had been reading Zen, or what?"

Gunadharma's suggestion was adopted, but modified. Feeling that a vast empty space would look a little *too* empty, Bodhidharma added three circular terraces, one upon the other. "If anyone asks, tell them the perfect forms represent progression towards the perfection of Nirvana," he sighed. "*Arupadhatu* is No-Form, so Form must follow theology."

The sculptors were all hard at work when a convoy arrived, led by the Princess' chamberlain. He bowed to Bodhidharma and placed a letter in his hands. Since Post-it notes had not yet been invented, the letter was written on lontar leaf, covered with the elaborate Javanese script:

"*To Reverend Master Bodhidharma,*
    Greetings.
    I ordered eight Buddha statues for my courtyard, but those fools at Bandung got mixed up and sent me eighty. I am keeping eight and am sending the rest to you. Consider them a permanent loan. Put them somewhere on that hill, and we will call it Boro-budur, since it contains 'Borrowed Buddhas'. Ha-ha, that's a pun."

"What are we going to do with *seventy-two* statues?" Bodhidharma wailed.

There was nowhere to put them except on the circular terraces, but it worked out surprisingly well: thirty-two on the first circle, twenty-four on the next and sixteen on the top, conveniently using up all seventy-two. "Multiples of eight," Gunadharma sighed. "At least the Chinese would think it lucky."

So did the local villagers; they flocked to the site and placed offerings of food and flowers before the statues. In vain did Bodhidharma explain that Buddha had passed into Nirvana long ago, had extinguished the Self, and was hardly in need of rice and sambal. But, the villagers were appalled.

"Then why are there statues? It would be impious not to make offerings!"

Bodhidharma realised he would need time to educate the peasants. However, the food created a problem: dogs came to eat, and birds came to peck. And, you know dogs. They claim territory by leaving urine marks. A territory with *daily* food was valuable, so in no time the bases of the statues were... be-pissed.

Bodhidharma was away in Jogjakarta, so it was left to his disciples to solve the problem.

"What can we do?" the monks scratched their heads. "We can't chase them away. We who beg for our food hardly have the right to deny these hungry creatures their little allotment!"

"What if we just raise the statues on high plinths?"

Gunadharma shook his head. "No. They had already been dowelled to the floor. But we can build curbs around them... round ones, to go with the circular terraces. Form follows form."

But when Bodhidharma returned, he was appalled.

"Why have you put Lord Buddha in a bathtub?" he cried.

Everybody looked at the statues. Too late, they realised the circular curbs *did* look rather like Japanese hot tubs. Or, maybe Jacuzzis.

"What will the Princess say when she sees this?" Bodhidharma wailed. "Can't you build something that doesn't *look* so much like a tub?"

Just then, three birds perching on a Buddha head dropped their droppings, making a revolting mess.

"So much for curbs!" Bodhidharma grumbled. "Can we add pavilions to cover the statues?"

Buddha bath.

"A square pavilion won't go with a circular base," somebody remarked.

Gunadharma cried out, "I know! We'll extend the circle upwards and turn them into little stupas!"

"Then how do we see the statues?" Bodhidharma demanded.

"Cut some holes. Diamond-shaped holes, like the Diamond Sutra!" Gunadharma exclaimed.

When the Princess came for a visit, she was none too pleased. "I didn't expect a bunch of peek-a-boo Buddhas," she frowned.

"Your Highness, it is *symbolic*," said Gunadharma, bowing low. "It symbolises the fact that the Dharma is not easy to understand. It takes effort to see the Truth."

She glared at him. "You got a glib tongue, you. Ever thought of practicing law?"

Then she looked at the centre of the topmost circle, which had been left empty, and asked the question that everybody had been dreading. "What goes there?"

Everyone looked at Gunadharma, who stammered, "Your Highness, we intend to put *nothing* there. Nirvana is defined by negatives. It is no-birth, no-death, no-form, no-stain…"

The Princess snapped, "How would you like no-head?"

Gunadharma cringed. "Maybe we can put a little stupa there…"

"Little?" the Princess snarled. "How can it be *little?* That would be insulting. I want a big one. A huge one. A stupendous stupa! A stupefying stupa!"

"A stupid stupa," Gunadharma objected. "Too much weight will squash the hill again…"

"Looks like *somebody* will get squashed pretty soon," the Princess said, in a voice of thunder.

Never argue with royalty.

Sure enough, not long after the stupendous stupa was added, the terraces started to bulge outwards again. The Princess had enough. "I'm converting to Jainism," she announced. "Too bad it is non-violent, otherwise I'd hang the whole lot of you."

This, then, was the sad story of Borobudur and Prambanan – starting off as a single building, ripped apart, then subject to a series of chaotic changes. This secret was transmitted through generations of Javanese architects, down the ages. Of course, they said nothing to the Dutch colonists. But when Indonesia became independent, President Sukarno was told; so was his successor Suharto – all the way to the present government. *All had sworn to keep the secret.*

Why? For a start, if UNESCO found out, they would insist on reclassifying the two monuments as a *single* World Heritage Site, instead of two. That meant the authorities wouldn't be able to charge admission twice. Or worse, UNESCO might downgrade both to World Heritage Dumpsites.

But, worse than that – oh, far worse – was the *embarrassment.* Java had always seen itself as the cultural and political leader of Indonesia, the most advanced and sophisticated of all the islands. How embarrassing would it be to admit its great architectural achievements were the results of bits and pieces thrown together, in a series of ad-hoc decisions, a complete mishmash!

How Aceh would snigger! How the Sumatrans would sneer! How the Balinese would laugh!

And yet, ironically, the man that Borobudur sought to honour would not have cared. Buddha taught that everything is transitory, so the notion of building a great monument would have struck him as absurd. And, as for it being a mishmash of odds and ends – Buddha would have laughed and said, "You want to see a mishmash? Take a look inside my begging bowl."

09 WHO'S THE NAUGHTY ONE?

The twenty temples at Khajuraho, Madhya Pradesh, have long been celebrated for their architectural beauty and imposing size, but even more so for the erotic sculptures mounted on their exterior facades, some of which are so explicit they would make *Playboy* magazine blush.

But now, it appears that those sculptures might have been... *fakes.*

Or, is the fakery itself faked?

A temple in Khajuraho.

In 2011, the staff of the *Daily Delhi* were preparing to move to a bigger office. Whilst clearing the archives, they came across a small safe. As the key was long lost, they cut it open and found an old envelope, postmarked 'Bombay, 8 May, 1912' that contained a sealed package. A covering letter asked the newspaper to keep the package for twenty years, after which they were to open it and publish the contents. The letter was signed: 'A devoted reader'.

It was a tribute to the long-dead staff of 1912 that they did not peek inside the package, nor throw the whole thing into the rubbish bin, but instead kept it in the safe. However, they plainly forgot all about it. Since the due date had long passed, the staff broke the package open.

And, that sent shock waves through the government...

The sealed package contained the 'confessions' of one Bruce MacIlk, a young Scottish sculptor who arrived in British India around 1850 to seek his fortunes. He was dismayed to find that his services were not needed. Local Indian sculptors had learnt to imitate western styles and were supplying all the fake Greco-Roman statuary needed by colonists; and of course, they were doing it at a fraction of his costs. Out of work, he was persuaded 'by deceptive words' into buying a guesthouse in Khajuraho, only to find the place deserted when he arrived. "My guesthouse was in good condition," he wrote. "But of actual guests there was nary a one." He had thought Khajuraho was a busy town with many travellers, but found out too late, that it was located in the middle of nowhere.

He wrote: *"… Despondent, I visited the Hindoo [sic] temples nearby, for they were the only things of note in that God-forsaken place. They were discovered only recently and seldom visited. One day, exhausted under the hot sun, I found refuge under a date palm, there being no one living nearby that can offer the shelter of a roof. I fell asleep, and perhaps I had been long without any female companionship, my dreams were of a particularly vivid and sensual sort. When I awoke, I glanced at the nearest temple and saw that some of the niches were empty, the statuary having fallen off long ago. Suddenly I was visited by a thought: I can make my dreams come true and restore my fortunes as well!"*

MacIlk found the ancient quarries that supplied sandstone for the temples, and transported several chunks to his guesthouse, where he built a shed to house them. Then –

"… at considerable danger to myself, I climbed up to the empty niches and took careful measurements of the spaces available."

He then spent the next month carving sculptures –

"… of the most erotic and naughty sort, with deities engaged in postures which even now I blush to describe. It made me laugh to think that, even as the Indians are churning out fake Greek gods, a Scotsman is now churning out fake Hindoo goddesses!"

The text went on to describe how he 'aged and eroded' the surfaces to make them seem old, wrapped them in protective sackcloth and hired workers from Jhansi to hoist them into place.

"… I chose Jhansi since it was some distance from Khajuraho – I did not want the locals to know. The workers could not see the statues, for they were bundled up in protective cloth. I told them

I was from the Department of Antiquities, and the statues had been 'repaired' and must be placed in their old positions. I feared they may ask questions, but fortunately, these ignorant fellows did not doubt the words of a pukka sahib..."

After the workers left, MacIlk removed the sackcloth and took careful photographs of 'my beauties' which he sent to newspapers in Britain and India, announcing the discovery of 'Erotic Tantric Sculptures' at Khajuraho. He also emphasised his 'clean and comfortable hostel' was just five minutes away.

Results were gratifying. Within days, an Anglican clergyman arrived from Delhi, demanding to see these 'pagan filth' in order to 'make a report to the Church'. When he asked why they were not noticed earlier, MacIlk pointed out that there were thousands of statues, and obviously T.S. Burt, the man who first rediscovered the temples in 1838, had simply missed them. Within a week his guesthouse was overflowing with Victorian gentlemen (no women) and MacIlk started building an annex. By the end of the year, he had raised room rates and was 'raking it in'.

"... I built a new studio far from the guesthouse, enclosed by walls, with only a clerestory window for light. Whilst my staff took care of my guests, I hid in the studio, chipping away happily. My success spurred me to push my limits of invention, although I must admit, when I tried some of these positions with my darling Radha I nearly broke my back!"

It seemed MacIlk did find 'female companionship' after all.

"... Visitors invariably say they are 'scholars' and 'antiquarians' who are interested in art and architecture, but what rubbish!

"… some of these positions… nearly broke my back!"

They spend five minutes studying the buildings and the rest of the day staring at my beauties, binoculars glued to their faces. When they leave, their eyes are bulging, and I swear their trousers too."

The text ended with MacIlk explaining – now in his eighties and having made his fortune – he wished to confess all: *"… so that in two decades, the world would know of my artistic triumphs. By then, I shall be dead and laughing in my grave."*

The 'MacIlk Confessions' was a bombshell. *Daily Delhi* submitted the documents to the government. The President formed a secret committee to consider the matter – codenamed *The Kama Slutra Project*.

The committee summoned editors of major publications in India, and after swearing them to secrecy, showed them the 'Confessions' and asked for their opinions: "*Should we go public?*"

The *Calcutta Cutter* screamed, "No way. This is so embarrassing!"

The *Mumbai Mumble* opined, "Our tourism will collapse..."

The *Bombay Bombast* muttered, "And they call Bollywood films indecent?"

Everybody censured the *Daily Delhi* for forgetting the letter for so long, "... thus leaving India with an embarrassing reputation." The committee concluded the MacIlk fakes must be destroyed, but this was stopped short by the *Daily Delhi,* asking: "What if the 'MacIlk Confessions' is itself – faked?"

"Huh?"

The editor of Daily Delhi explained, "What if the statues are in fact genuine, but someone, either MacIlk or a prankster using his name, made up the whole story about faking the statues and installing them? If so, the statues are national treasures and their destruction would be unthinkable!"

"Why would anyone do such a thing?" an editor demanded.

"Well, it must be admitted that the British can have a rather odd sense of humour..." the *Daily Delhi* said. "One can imagine some old duffer chuckling to himself, even on his deathbed, thinking about the storm his 'confessions' would stir up. What if we are now falling into his little trap?"

The committee, caught in a dilemma, formed a task force comprising of scientists, historians and art experts to investigate the matter. Alas, to date their results were inconclusive.

As it turned out, there *was* a Bruce MacIlk, who *did* own a guesthouse at Khajuraho; but as there were no surviving samples of his writing, handwriting experts had nothing to compare the 'MacIlk Confessions" with. The guesthouse itself had long vanished, replaced by a modern shopping mall.

There were few records of the construction of the Khajuraho temples. Little is known, beyond the fact that most of them were built between 950 and 1050 AD. The Arab traveller Ibn Battuta, passing through the region in the fourteenth century, did mention 'dreadful filth' but it was not clear he was referring to Khajuraho at all.

Old photographs of the Khajuraho temples taken before the 1850s were so grey and blurry they told nothing. Sketches by artists were so obviously wrong in their details they were useless.

Since radiocarbon dating does not work on stone, the surfaces of the erotic statues were minutely examined under microscope. Some experts claimed they spotted modern tool marks; others asserted they were consistent with ancient tools.

Art historians were even more divided. Much attention was focused on the '… nearly broke my back' statue-group – for the lower legs of the woman in the middle were impossibly long.

"How long does a woman's legs need to be?" an art critic scoffed.

"Long enough to reach the ground!" another critic gleefully answered, quoting Abraham Lincoln.

"A classically-trained sculptor would never make such a blunder," one pointed out. "Therefore, it *cannot* be done by MacIlk. It must be genuine!"

"Are you saying Indian sculptors had no sense of proportion?" came an angry rebuttal. "More likely this MacIlk *deliberately* made this mistake, just so the viewer would think it *wasn't* made by him!"

"I think he left it as a clue – he's pulling *our* legs!"

Argue, argue, argue...

Everyone was stumped, and UNESCO threatened to withdraw the World Heritage Site status from the temples.

Are the erotic statues real and the 'MacIlk Confessions' a hoax? Or, are the statues fake and the 'MacIlk Confessions' real? In frustration, the *Daily Delhi* snarled, "What is real? What is unreal? This is starting to resemble the movie *Rashamon*. We should invite Kurosawa to come help us, but alas, he's dead."

So, who's the naughty one?

Dear reader, you decide. Was it the ancient sculptors, who carved those naughty scenes? Or, was MacIlk being naughty, creating those erotic sculptures and writing his 'Confessions'? Or, was it an unknown prankster, naughtily pretending to be MacIlk?

Are the statues fakes? Or is the fakery itself faked?

Come to think of it, what about this book you are now reading...?

10 **THE ONION DOMES OF RUSSIA**

Onion domes are perhaps the most distinctive features of Russian architecture, appearing on almost every church throughout the land. Yet its origins are strange. Russian Orthodoxy was rooted in Greek Orthodoxy, transmitted to Kiev by the Byzantine Empire – but Byzantine domes were low-slung and shallow. So, how did Byzantine flattish saucer-domes mutate into tall, bulbous onion domes in Russia?

Around 980 AD, Grand Prince Vladimir of Kiev decided to renounce paganism in favor of monotheism. Perhaps, he got tired of praying to so many different deities. "One god, one prayer, saves time!" he allegedly declared. In search of the ideal 'One-Stop-Prayer', he went shopping for a suitable monotheistic creed.

He rejected Judaism, "I'll be damned if I'm going to wear little curly ringlets!"

Next, he turned down Roman Catholicism, "Who can remember all those catechisms?"

An exuberant sprouting of onion domes on St Basil's Cathedral, Moscow.

This reduced candidates to two: Islam and Greek Orthodoxy. He sent emissaries to Bulgaria – recently converted to Islam by Ibn Fadlan – and to Constantinople, capital of the Byzantine Empire, inviting both to send missionaries to Kiev, where each would build a house of worship in which he could study their respective teachings.

The Byzantine Emperor, Basil II, responded eagerly, seeing a golden opportunity to make allies of the unruly and troublesome Kievan Rus'. He sent a huge delegation headed by a bishop, priests and a team of masons. They arrived at the end of 987 AD and started at once to build a church on the banks of the Dnieper.

However, the Bulgarians were in a fix. Being recent converts themselves, they did not feel qualified to preach, so they sent a message to Baghdad. However, the caliphate was undergoing a power struggle, and the ruler At-Ta'i could only send one Imam, some assistants and a mason, Ibrahim. They arrived much later than their Christian rivals; and Grand Prince Vladimir, sensing trouble if he let the two religions get at each other, wisely decreed the mosque be built on the *other* side of the river.

"If they want to kill each other, at least they'll have to swim first," he said resignedly.

Alas, the unfortunate Imam never made it back to Baghdad, for on the way home he died of sorrow and disappointment. It was left to Ibrahim, the mason, to report to the Caliph what happened:

"... I beg your Sublime Highness to understand the difficulties in working with the local masons, for they are drunk half the time and crazy the other half. It was with the greatest difficulty that I taught them how to build arches and vaults, while dizzy from the smell of vodka in their breaths... Indeed, I had to secretly hire a few infidel [i.e. Christian] masons from the opposite banks to come over and moonlight, or else I would have died.

When the base of the dome was reached, I fell sick from exhaustion, and whilst in bed I prayed that the drunken masons would follow my drawings correctly. After my fever abated, I staggered back to the site and a most miserable dome met my eyes. These drunken fools had simply laid each brick

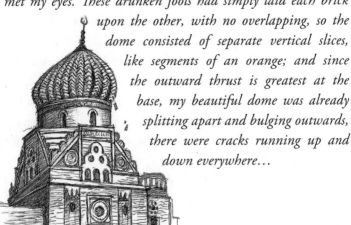

upon the other, with no overlapping, so the dome consisted of separate vertical slices, like segments of an orange; and since the outward thrust is greatest at the base, my beautiful dome was already splitting apart and bulging outwards, there were cracks running up and down everywhere..."

Bulging happens when masons do not bond their stone courses properly. This dome in Cairo collapsed in 1882.

... I was panic-stricken, for Grand Prince Vladimir was due to return to Kiev in three days, and there was simply no time to rebuild the dome. I had to rely on ad hoc ingenuity. I bought a length of iron chain from the local shipwright and wound it tightly around the bulging dome, like a corset, so as to prevent it from bulging further and collapsing entirely. Then I slathered on thick layers of plaster to hide the chain and smooth the outline, all the while ignoring the jeers from the Christian infidels across the river.

Grand Prince Vladimir returned and spent the first day at the Byzantine Church. I disguised himself and hung out outside the church, busily flapping my ears. By now, I had picked up a little of their uncouth tongue, and can follow some of their conversations. While I listened, a great commotion arose from within the church. All Vladimir's women were weeping and crying, 'Ah! What will happen to us? Where will we go?' I think the Christian priest have just told the Grand Prince he will be allowed to keep only one wife, hence the lamentation of all the others.

As Grand Prince Vladimir had 800 wives and concubines, your Sublime Highness could imagine the racket. The women were not comforted when told they could enter a convent – they thought it was some sort of hen-coop. The next day, the Grand Prince made a visit to the mosque, followed by 800 gloomy women, most of whom were obliged to sit outside due to shortage of space.

The Grand Prince stood in front and stared long at my embarrassing dome, bulbous as an onion, but I could not tell whether he liked it or not... At last he entered, and sat on a sumptuous carpet facing our beloved Imam, who taught him the holy words of the Prophet, translated by a Bulgarian assistant. Since I am only a humble mason, I sat some distance away, and could only hear the gentle murmur of the Imam and the translator, but I saw the Grand Prince nod and say, 'Good! I need not send them to a hen-coop or convent, whatever that is.'

They spoke in low voices, and I was getting a little drowsy, but suddenly I heard the Grand Prince exclaim, 'No wine? Then what about vodka?' There was more murmuring from the Imam, and then the Prince yelled, 'No vodka? Then what can we drink?'... And then, 'WATER? Are you crazy?'

The Prince arose, his face like thunder, and stalked out of the mosque, whilst our poor Imam collapsed weeping. The next day, we were told to leave. But as we sadly packed our belongings, the Grand Prince came, followed by Greek priests. I saw Grand Prince Vladimir point to my dome and say, 'Put a couple of that on your church.'

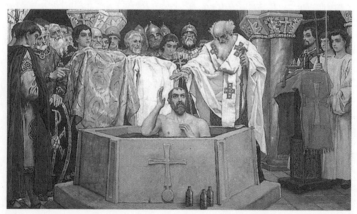

Baptism of Grand Prince Vladimir of Kiev, by water and vodka.

The Greeks sneered, 'My Lord, it is a drunken dome built by drunken idiots!'

'Exactly,' Vladimir said, with a beatific smile. 'That's why I like it.'"

Wisely, the Greek Orthodox delegation decided that an unorthodox dome was a small price to spread Greek Orthodoxy throughout the land, and so added an onion dome – probably wood – on top of their flat saucer-dome. Although this first church had not survived, it provided a pattern for all subsequent Russian churches. Onion domes were here to stay.

It is ironic that a misshapen dome, built by drunken masons on behalf of a religion that abhorred alcohol, ended up being the iconic emblem of a rival faith. But, the history of architecture can go strange places and take odd turns.

As Grand Prince Vladimir said, "Architects are crazy, even when sober."

11 ANGKOR WHAT?

Angkor Wat in Cambodia is one of the great monuments of the world. Each year millions of visitors traipse through its cloisters, admire its bas-reliefs and tremblingly ascend its incredibly steep staircases. Yet very few visitors pause to consider – or are even aware of – its oddity.

It is facing the wrong way.

Other monuments in the Angkor complex face east. East is the direction of sunrise, associated with rebirth and renewal. By contrast, west is sunset: decay, death, 'gone west'. It is no surprise that ancient Khmers always oriented their temples facing east.

But Angkor Wat faces *west*.

How did the largest religious monument in the world get built ass-backwards?

Laymen think it is easy to find east. "Look for the sunrise, stupid!" But in reality, it is not that simple.

The sun rises due east – *precisely* east – only twice a year. On Spring Equinox, it does indeed rise exactly east, but

Angkor Wat – built ass-backwards.

on successive days it rises ever more to the north, creeping to the left little by little, until it rises twenty-three degrees north of east on Summer Solstice. Then the sun retraces its steps, each day rising more and more to the right, until Autumn Equinox when it rises due east once again. After that, the sun continues its rise further to the right, until Winter Solstice when it reaches its southernmost extremity (twenty-three degrees south of east). Finally, the sun reverses again and rises successively northwards, back to Spring Equinox.

So how do you know *where* due east is? Easy – wait for an Equinox and watch the sunrise. But, how do you know *when* the Equinox is? Easy – wait until the sun rises due east.

In short, it is a chicken-and-egg problem. The trouble is that the sun transits through the Equinoxes left to right, or right to left, without pausing, so it is nearly impossible to tell *which* day an Equinox actually is. The only sure way is to wait for the Summer Solstice – easy to detect since the sun reaches its northernmost limit – and draw a line of sight to the sunrise; then wait six months for the Winter Solstice and do the same. The midpoint of the two limits, then, is due east.

It was a hassle. Worse, since the exact direction was so important, every Angkor monument had to have "due east" determined anew. The temples were spaced far apart, so trying to copy-cat an existing axis from one temple to another was dangerous. Given the many steps needed, cumulative errors could lead to disaster. It was done only once, and when the completed temple was found to be (horrors!) *five* degrees off due east, the hapless architect was hurled down the staircase of doom.

Suryavarman II mounted the throne in 1113 AD. After subduing all his nearer enemies, he embarked on his grand monument, Angkor Wat. It consisted of a huge central tower, representing sacred Mount Meru, surrounded by lesser towers at each corner, linked by cloisters. More cloisters and galleries surrounded the complex, and finally, an outer moat. The primary axis of approach was over a grand causeway that crossed the moat, penetrated through successive cloisters, up to the central tower. It was to be the grandest monument ever attempted; and of course, *it was to face east.*

The Chief Architect, along with his Chief Mason and Chief Surveyor, set to work, clearing out a huge rectangular plot of approximately the right size – and waited.

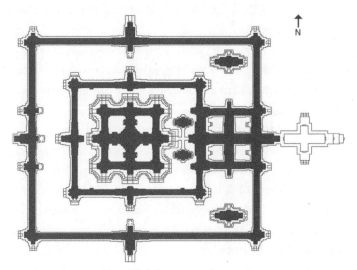

Angkor Wat, as originally planned.

"What is the matter?" the King snarled, as he visited the site and found that, although much of the materials had arrived, no actual construction had yet started – not even the foundation.

"Your Majesty, we had just measured the midsummer sunrise," the Chief Surveyor reported. "Now we are waiting for midwinter."

"What? You are going to sit around for the next six months doing nothing?"

"Yes, Sire. That's the only way we can be sure of finding due east!"

"You builders are all the same," the King growled. "Always demanding Extension of Time!"

As Suryavarman II sulked in his palace, a Chinese merchant came to the rescue.

"Your Majesty!" he said, bowing low. "My humble name is Fa-Ming. My great-great-great-great-great-great-great-grandfather, Faxian, visited your illustrious court centuries ago!"

"Nobody's *that* great," Suryavarman snarled.

"True," said Fa-Ming, a little crestfallen. "All the same, I believe I have a great solution to your problem!" A servant pulled off a piece of silk and revealed an odd-looking device. It looked like a Monopoly board with a metal spoon stuck to its middle. Ceremoniously, Fa-Ming set it on a table, and slowly rotated the board...

The spoon stood still! No matter how the board was turned, the handle of the spoon always pointed to the same direction. The King stared at it in astonishment, then with suspicion.

"Point-South-Needle".

"How is it done?" the King asked. He lifted the board and looked underneath, but could not discover any trickery. He tilted and twisted the board this way and that, but always, the spoon slowly drifted back to the same orientation.

"Sire, we call it a 'Point-South-Needle'. We Chinese invented it a millennium ago. It is made of a material called 'lodestone' and the handle of the spoon *always* points to the south. And if you know south, you will automatically know all the other directions!"

It was of course a magnetic compass, and it became the King's favourite toy. He carried it around everywhere, putting it here, turning it there, and watched fascinated, as the spoon slowly and majestically resumed its correct direction.

"Why is it shaped like a spoon?" he asked Fa-Ming.

"We Chinese like to eat," Fa-Ming shrugged.

Suryavarman II argued, "Then it should be shaped like a *chopstick*, no?"

"Then how can one tell which end is which?' Fa-Ming asked, logically.

The King brought the compass to the worksite and showed it to the Chief Architect, Chief Mason and Chief Surveyor. Predictably, everyone was impressed.

"There you are!" the King said, triumphantly." No need to wait for Winter Solstice! With this device you immediately know where south is. So, to orientate my temple, turn left a right-angle from the handle, and that's that!"

A week later, Suryavarman II went on a military campaign to conquer the Chams, leaving his compass at the work site. Two days later, the setting out of the temple started in earnest. The Chief Architect, Chief Mason and Chief Surveyor brought the compass out from storage and carefully set it down on the ground. Slowly the spoon rotated, and came to rest.

Everyone stared.

Everyone scratched their heads.

"That can't be right," the Chief Architect muttered.

"Not right at all," the Chief Surveyor opined.

"Last time, this thing pointed to that clump of coconuts," the Chief Mason noted. "But today, it is pointing directly *away* from them!"

"I think this device is bust!"

"Damn the Chinese and their bloody inventions."

"So, what do we do?"

What happened was – a magnetic polarity reversal.

For those geologically-challenged: our planet has a core of molten iron, slowly sloshing about, and as it spins it generates a magnetic field. In fact, planet Earth is a magnet, like those you stick on your refrigerator door, only bigger.

But every few thousand millennia, Earth's polarity reverses. North becomes south and south becomes north. Nobody knows why the Earth does this – maybe out of sheer boredom.

Magnetic polarity reversal was first revealed by Project Magnet in 1955, which towed a magnetometer back and forth across the Atlantic Ocean. Running across the middle of the Atlantic is a huge gash in the seabed, a giant crack where tectonic plates are pulling apart, with lava rising up from underneath. In the lava are tiny needles of iron which automatically orientate themselves to the Earth's magnetic field – *as it existed at that time.* On contact with icy water the lava freezes, trapping iron particles in fixed orientation. As more lava gushed out, more iron needles got frozen in place, forming band after band of solidified lava. As the Earth's magnetic field flip-flopped, each band showed a polarity the *reverse* of its neighbour. When the 'normal' and 'reverse' polarities are shown in black and white on a map, the effect looks like the hide of a zebra. With the astonishing

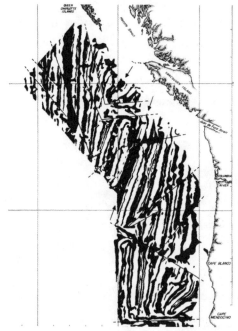

Zebra stripes under the Atlantic.

technology available nowadays, the last magnetic reversal could be pinpointed with accuracy – and as it turned out, it happened *exactly* when Angkor Wat was being set out.

"So, what do we do?" the Chief Mason whispered.

"Let's throw this stupid thing out!" the Chief Architect growled.

"Can't do that, the King will skin us alive!"

"But if we follow it, the temple will face west!" the Chief Surveyor objected.

"Well, maybe the King *intended* it to face west."

"He never actually specified which direction to face, did he?"

The Chief Architect scratched his head. "No, all he said was 'turn left a right-angle from the handle'."

"Maybe he meant 'turn right a left-angle from the handle'?" the Chief Mason ventured.

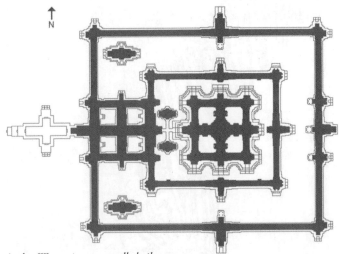

Angkor Wat, as it was actually built.

"No such thing as a 'left-angle'!" the Chief Architect said, huffily.

"Unfair to southpaws," muttered the Chief Mason, who was left-handed.

Not daring to delay any further, the three men decided to follow the King's instructions literally. Setting out proceeded... ending up with the temple facing west, not east.

The King returned in triumph, after vanquishing the Chams of Champa, in what came to be known as the Cham Offensive. In a good mood he visited the construction site; but what with the Chief Mason's blocks of stone everywhere, and the setting-out strings placed by the Chief Surveyor zigzagging all over the place, he failed to notice anything amiss. He had a poor sense of direction anyway – the type who had to turn the map upside-down if he happened to be heading south, otherwise he could not figure out which highway exit to take.

"Sire, about the orientation..." the Chief Architect ventured to whisper to the King.

"Don't bother me now!" the King said, impatiently. He yelled at the Chief Sculptor, "I don't like that Naga. Why has it only seven heads? I want nine!"

"Sire, I just want to confirm the temple is orientated as you wished..."

"Hey! Why is that devata so scrawny? Give her bigger breasts!"

So, they never told the King.

After many years of work, the temple stood complete. Very pleased, Suryavarman II arrived a day before the consecration, so he could look over and enjoy his masterpiece in private, without hordes of monks and Brahmins all over the place. He admired the intricate floral scrolls, inspected the Ramayana, and salivated over the devatas, dressed in extravagant headdresses and very little else.

Finally, satisfied, he returned to the entrance portal, preparing to depart. But, as he stood on the topmost step, gloating over this great achievement, a shaft of light pierced his eyes and made him blink.

It was the setting sun.

Confused, he squinted at the horizon. He is facing *east,* surely, so how could the evening sun be *right in front* of him? Did he stay so long that night came and went, and he didn't even notice?

But as the truth dawned (even though the day didn't), his face grew pink, then red, then purple...

"How can you let it happen?" he screamed as the Chief Architect, Chief Mason and Chief Surveyor cringed and grovelled on the ground before him.

"Sire! We did exactly as you told us!"

They brought out the compass. "See, your Majesty! We did as you bade us – turn left a right-angle from the handle of the spoon!"

The King stared at the compass. There could be no mistake. The handle pointed to the wrong direction. "It's a Chinese conspiracy," he whispered. To the three men he said,

"I made a mistake. I admit it was my fault. I put my faith in the infernal device… but all the same…"

He glared at them. "… All the same… *you should have known better!*"

One by one, they were hurled off the staircase of doom, landing in a broken heap at the bottom.

Young architects kindly take note:

- If you follow instructions, you're dead; and
- If you *don't* follow instructions, you're dead.

Staircase of doom.

My advice is to switch to a less dangerous profession, such as smuggling heroin.

The King tried to salvage things – at least save appearances – by opening a new portal on the east side, but he died of heartbreak before it was completed. He was succeeded by his cousin Dharanindravarman II, whose rule was weak, mainly because nobody could pronounce his name. In 1177, Angkor was attacked and sacked by the Chams, thirsting for revenge. At least they were not so foolish as to trust some new-fangled device, but simply followed the road signs.

AFTERWORD

The effect of the magnetic polarity reversal was far greater than the misalignment of a monument. It had serious, far-reaching, *global* impact…

In 1492, a fellow named Christopher Columbus jumped on board a ship, the *Santa Maria*.

"Where to, Sir?" the helmsman asked.

"China. I promised Her Majesty to get some Oolong Tea."

The helmsman nodded wisely. "China is to the east."

"Everybody knows *that*,' Columbus said, huffily. He consulted his pocket compass, and pointed, "*That* way."

12 SETTING THE RECORD STRAIGHT

When I started on this book, I put out an appeal for interesting cases on my website. The response had been overwhelming. Of them all, none was as mysterious as that offered by an Italian named Bruno, which, he admitted, was a false name.

"I cannot email you," he wrote. "They will kill me. Come to Pisa."

I thought I was dealing with a nutcase, but in 2013, during a visit to Florence, I finally took up his offer and made a side trip to Pisa. As Bruno refused to give me an address, we met outside the south transept of the Pisa cathedral, within sight of the Leaning Tower. Bruno turned out to be a thin, dark, morose man, but I was not prepared for his huge, saucer-like dark glasses which hid half his face.

We shook hands and I asked him what the deep dark secret was. Without a word he took me by the hand and dragged me out to the grass, directly facing the Tower.

"Close your eyes and move from side to side a little," he told me.

I objected, "Why? I don't want to look like an idiot!"

"Just do it, please?" he implored.

I did as he bade me, but when I opened my eyes again, I felt a strange but fleeting sense of disorientation. For an instant, it seemed the Leaning Tower was actually *straight*, and everything else was tilted slightly to the left. I shook my head in bewilderment, and in a moment, everything was normal again – there was the world, the ground was flat, with the Tower leaning to the right.

Bruno looked at me with a sardonic smile. "Ah, you see it, do you not?"

"What happened? Is this some sort of trick? For a moment the Tower looked straight!"

"This is the deep, dark secret. The Leaning Tower does *not* lean. *It is straight.* It is everything else around it that is leaning the other way."

I stared at him.

Bruno smiled sourly. "Look, how do you know what is up, and what is down? There is this little thing inside your ears, like – how you say – a spirit level, and it tells you where the gravity is, yes? It tells you if you are upright or upside down, *yes*? But it is crude, it does not detect small angles. Otherwise, every time you tilt your head, you get seasick."

The Tower of Pisa, correctly displayed.

"By your logic we should all be walking around like drunks."

With an operatic gesture, Bruno pointed two fingers at my eyes, as if to poke them out.

"It is your eyes, Signor, that orientate you. You see the houses, the streets, the trees; your eyes tell you these are vertical, and your brain *knows* they are vertical, so you believe so. *But eyes can be fooled.* You see those funfairs where they build flat streets, but the 'houses' on the sides are tilted, so everybody inside walk around tilted, as though they are trying to climb a slope?

"So that is the secret: everything around here – the Duomo, the nearby houses, even the flagpoles – are all tilted to the north. Only the Tower is truly vertical. Your eyes fooled you because your brain assumed the surrounding is 'normal' and therefore the Tower is tilted to the south. But just now, with your eyes closed, you relied only on your inner ears – your 'spirit levels' – and you righted yourself. And when you looked again, for a moment you saw the truth – until your brain lied to you again."

I found a piece of string and tied a pencil to one end; and held this makeshift plumb line up against the Tower. True enough, the Tower *WAS* vertical! But the effect on Bruno was startling; he nearly screamed and yanked me back inside the Duomo. "Don't let them see you do that!" he whispered.

"Why not?"

"This is a secret. Do you not understand?" Bruno implored.

Just then, a tour bus disgorged a mass of noisy Chinese tourists. As we watched, they gleefully scampered to the Tower, like iron filings to a magnet.

"But if the ground is sloping, how come nobody noticed?" I protested. "The masons of the Duomo had plumb lines and they could easily have built the cathedral straight, instead of tilted!"

"The cathedral *was* built straight. The tilting started *after* it was completed. You know plate tectonics? Italy is made of many little sub-plates, and when the cathedral was nearing completion the Milan Plate started to push south, into the Pisa Plate. A gentle hump was formed. The ground at Via Ugo Rindi is flat, but south of it, the ground starts to tilt; at Via Contessa it is 2 degrees. In the vicinity of the Duomo, it reached 4 degrees. Then it flattens to a ridge at Via Risorti, and after that it slopes down the other way, down to the River Arno. Everything on the ridge got tilted, but never more than 4 degrees, so life went on as usual," Bruno explained.

"And when the mason started on the Tower, they used their plumb lines to build a properly vertical campanile. They didn't realise it would *look* tilted because it would contrast with its surroundings."

Peeping out to the lawn, we saw tourists all over the grass, taking photos of each other, doing the usual silly things like pretending to 'push' against the Tower or 'hold' it in their open hands. Bruno eyed them sardonically. "Tourists! What do they know? They are here for ten minutes. They are happily fooled. Do you know why there is so much grass lawn and not a single pond or fountain in sight? Because that would give the game away! Do you now understand why the vendors sell only *canned* drinks, and never anything in a cup?"

I was flabbergasted. "You mean everyone in Pisa *knows*?"

"*Of course* everybody knows, but we say nothing. It is conspiracy. It is omertà. You know omertà? Everybody keeps quiet, like the Mafia. I found out, I tried to tell, then my phone was cut, my power turned off, I was fired from my job, and even my passport was revoked," Bruno said, bitterly.

"But what about the big effort to save the Tower, back in the nineties? They even tied steel cables from the Tower to hold it back, didn't they?"

"Do not be so naïve! Have you never heard of a PR stunt?"

"But why is it so important to keep it secret in the first place?"

"Ah! You see how depressed this town is, how we are so dependent on tourism. And the silly tourists, they want to see nothing else. Do they ever step inside the Duomo? *No.* Do they visit the Baptistry? *Never.* How about the beautiful Camposanto? They never even heard of it! It's only the Tower, Tower, that stupid *Leaning* Tower everyone wants to see. It is our only asset. If the world finds out and the tourists stop coming, we starve, we die! But you must tell the world. But be careful."

"Why?"

"There was a man who dropped weights from the Tower. The fool was only interested to see if they fell at the same *rate*. But the rest of Pisa saw something very different: the weights fell *parallel* to the Tower. They were terrified he would tell. So, they got the Inquisition to drag him in and threaten him with torture. They nearly killed him, to keep the secret!"

"Who was it?"

"Some guy named Galileo."

13 MAI PEN RAI

Visitors to Thailand are charmed by the Thai's easy-going friendliness, tolerance and their love of *sanuk* (fun). The first phrase the visitors learn is '*mai pen rai*', or 'it doesn't matter' – which captures this spirit of easy tolerance.

Yet the *mai pen rai* attitude can be annoying, exasperating and even alarming:

"You forgot my breakfast!"

"*Mai pen rai…*"

"Flight delayed ten hours!"

"*Mai pen rai…*"

"The train smashed into the terminal!"

"*Mai pen rai…*"

The origins of *mai pen rai* go way back – to a time when Thailand was Siam, and its centre was the Kingdom of Sukhothai. But even back then, not every Siamese was enchanted by *mai pen rai…*

Sukhothai today.

"*Mai pen rai! Always mai pen rai!* I'm so sick of that phrase!" yelled Prasert, the Royal Chancellor. He slammed a report down on the table. "Look at it! Three spelling errors in a single report!"

His wife, Mook, glanced sidelong at the document. She could not move her head, since she was having her hair dressed. "Darling, don't forget that our King invented the new alphabet just three years ago. Before then we were all struggling with Sanskrit. Be patient!"

"It's not the mistakes *per se* that riles me," her husband simmered. "It's the attitude. When I complained, all they did was shrug and say, *mai pen rai!*"

"Well, why *should* it matter?" Mook demanded. "So long as you understand it."

Prasert gave her a withering look, "It's the wrong attitude. Three bridges collapsed last month, and what did they say? '*Mai pen rai*, we'll just wade instead!' The city wall is crumbling, and what do they say? '*Mai pen rai*, we'll patch it up next season!' Five judges were caught taking bribes, and everybody just shrugged and said, '*Mai pen rai,* everybody does it!' How can you expect a country be run efficiently with such an attitude? How can we ever beat the Khmers?"

Whilst the Royal Chancellor fumed, the hairdresser inserted the last flower into Mook's hair.

"There! You're done!" she squealed and held a bronze mirror in front of Mook. "My! Aren't you pretty!"

Picking up her scissors, she bowed to Prasert, but as she sashayed her way out, she pinched the guard's buttocks. The guard grinned sheepishly.

Prasert lifted his eyebrows, "I must say, your hairdresser is rather frisky."

Mook laughed, "Actually, she's not really a she."

"What?" Prasert's eyebrows rose higher. "She is a *he*? One of those *katoeys* [transvestite]?"

"He – I mean she – wants to be a woman, so we treat her as one," Mook told her husband. "Do you know what I hear about some barbaric countries far to the west? There they call people like her 'sinners' and burn them alive. Here, we just giggle and say, '*mai pen rai*'. You call this the wrong attitude? Bah! It's the '*mai pen rai*' that makes us so tolerant and our country so pleasant to live in!"

"Tolerance is tolerable, up to a point," Prasert conceded. "But we can get *too* tolerant. We tolerate inefficiency, corruption and stupid mistakes!"

"Honey, what *is* the matter?" Mook demanded. "Today you're so agitated."

The Royal Chancellor sighed, "Alright, if truth be told, I'm worried. His Majesty had commanded a new temple to be built. A very grand one, and he wants it to be golden."

"You mean gilded? Can our treasury afford that much gold?"

"Don't be silly. What he wants are roof tiles that *look* golden, so the temple will glitter. I promised to see what can be done. I have entrusted the task to the Royal Potter, and I've asked the Royal Architect and Royal Carpenter to help."

"I'm sure those three clever men will think of something," Mook said, soothingly.

"Yeah. I bet those three rascals will invent some dirty brown glaze and call *that* 'golden'!"

Mook laughed, "Don't worry so much, dear." She kissed her husband and said, "*Mai pen rai.*"

At that precise moment, in another corner of the city, the 'three rascals' – Ba, Bo and Bu – were huddling in front of a kiln, getting increasingly worried. (Siamese generally had long, flowery names derived from Sanskrit which nobody, not even their own mothers, could remember. So, the three men were generally known by their nicknames: Ba, Bo and Bu respectively, in no particular order.)

"Will it work?" Ba whimpered.

"Keep praying," Bo sighed.

"Here goes…" Bu whispered, and opened the kiln. Using a tong, he pulled out a tray containing their latest experiments: fifty sample tiles, each glazed with a different formula; but the colours were all terrible, ranging from dirty brown to dingy greys.

"Cinnabar doesn't work," Ba sighed, glaring at the samples. "Nor does antimony."

"And we had already tried copper," Bo said in despair. "Makes the tile green instead!"

"These look like shit!" Bu shook his head. "What else can we try?"

"How about saffron?" Ba said, hopefully. "My wife said it gives food a golden glow. Maybe if we add it to the glaze, it would make the tile golden too?"

"Or, durian?" Bu volunteered. "Something bright yellow!"

"Turmeric?"

"Lemongrass!"

"Let's try them all. After all, what's there to lose?"

The next few days were terrible for their long-suffering wives, as the men ransacked their homes.

"Honey, did you take my fish sauce?" Ba's wife asked.

"Darling, what happened to our jackfruit?" Bo's wife demanded.

"Dearest, what *are* you doing with my rouge?" Bu's wife screeched.

One day, Bu opened the kiln, and one of the sample tiles caught everyone's eyes.

"Beautiful!" breathed Ba.

"Wonderful!" whispered Bo.

"Really, truly golden!" cried Bu.

Somehow, incredibly, they succeeded. Historians had long speculated what ingredients they had mixed into their glaze, as the formula had since been destroyed (for good reasons, as the reader will learn). But whatever they were, they worked.

Oh, it was beautiful. It was shiny and glittered like gold, but with a slightly reddish tinge, as if it was blushing shyly. The three men made a batch of these wonderful golden tiles and presented them to the Royal Chancellor, who was delighted and gave his approval.

Unfortunately, the 'three rascals' were so carried away, they forgot to test their product. This was to have a major consequence, not only to themselves, but the entire country as well…

Going into mass production, the Royal Pottery turned out huge batches of the new tiles, and the temple was roofed accordingly. It glittered so brightly the temple's roof could be seen for miles around. Everyone who came near it on a sunny day was bedazzled. Even before completion, pilgrims came from far and wide, and stood outside, lost in admiration. Everyone asked for the secret formula, but of course the three men weren't telling. "We are waiting until they invent copyright."

The altar was completed, and the statue of Buddha, seated in the meditation mudra, was respectfully set in place, surrounded by smaller statuettes, candles and incense burners.

An auspicious day was set for the Consecration. The Abbot arrived, along with dozens of monks and scores of young novices. The monks set up low platforms inside, with the Abbot seated centre, and the other monks to the side. A cord was stretched out from monk to monk as they prepared to recite the sutras. Everyone else – including Ba, Bo, and Bu – knelt on the floor, around a raised dais reserved for the Royal Chancellor, who was on his way.

And, it started to rain.

If you had ever experienced a tropical monsoon, you would know it did not *merely* rain; it arrived like the Niagara Falls on a blitzkrieg, like the Valkyries on a rampage. Within minutes, tons of water pounded furiously on the temple roof.

Whatever crazy ingredients the 'three rascals' had put into the glaze (durian, fish sauce?), the effect made the tiles exceedingly brittle. Under relentless pelting from the downpour, the tiles started to crack and shatter, breaking apart like a fusillade of fire-crackers.

Ba realised something was wrong when water started to trickle onto his head. Surprised, he looked up – only to see dozens of roof tiles overhead bursting apart, each hole spouting a stream of rainwater. Bo and Bu gasped, and tried to cover their heads as more water poured in.

The Abbot motioned to the novices. "Fetch buckets," he said simply. Glancing up, he added, "A *lot* of buckets."

Then, he returned to his calm meditation.

Prasert and his entourage were also caught in the rain. They were halfway to the new temple when the storm burst upon them. Both Prasert and Mook's palanquins were roofed, but everyone else got drenched.

"Excellency, shall we turn back?" his chamberlain asked.

The Royal Chancellor peered out of his palanquin, looked up into the heavens and shook his head. "We're already halfway there," he said, logically. "It's raining ahead and raining behind. Forward or backward, we'll get equally wet, so we may as well proceed."

As novices frantically ran to and fro, putting buckets and pails under every leaking point, the three men prostrated themselves before the Abbot, who continued to sit serenely in the lotus position.

"*Ajarn*! What shall we do?" Ba cried.

"His Excellency will boil us alive!" Bo wept.

"Please protect us!" Bu wailed.

The Abbot sighed and opened his eyes, "Perhaps you should get ready for your *next* reincarnation."

"No! No! No!" Ba cried.

"Not yet! Please save us!" Bo wept.

"We are not ready to die yet!" Bu wailed.

The Abbot sighed again. Then, he stood up and started to enumerate the Eightfold Path:

"*Right View:* from what I see, you three rascals are doomed.
Right Resolve: I will try to save you.
Right Speech: I am going to scold you.
Right Livelihood: your careers are probably over…

Right Effort: you had made commendable efforts, but –

Right Mindfulness: you messed up because you were brainless.

Right Meditation: I had meditated upon the matter and now, it's time for – *Right Action!"*

Grabbing a pail filled with rainwater from a passing novice, the Abbot splashed it over all three men. Whilst they gasped in astonishment, water running down their faces, the Abbot took another full bucket and handed it to them. "Make a virtue out of necessity. Splash me."

The Royal Chancellor arrived at the temple. Sodden, his entourage brought his palanquin into the porch and there he dismounted, with Mook following. But –

From within the temple came strange noises, like a troop of elephants rampaging, or a flock of *kinnaris* screeching. *What on earth was going on?*

Two novices greeted him and (hesitantly) opened the door, and Prasert stepped into complete mayhem. His first impression was that everybody had gone mad. Monks, novices, workmen and peasants were running around, grabbing buckets of water from the floor and splashing each other, screaming and whooping, whilst overhead roof tiles exploded like popcorn. As he stared, the Abbot came up to him, holding a bucket. "Your Excellency. Water is pure, cleansing and life-giving. May I have the honour of giving you its blessing?"

"Blessing?" Prasert stared. "What…"

Before he could finish his sentence, the Abbot upended the bucket of rainwater over him.

"Gaaahh..." the Royal Chancellor gasped, water streaming down his head and drenching his robe.

The Abbot took another bucket and held it out to Prasert. Dazed, Prasert took it mechanically. There was a moment of silence whilst everyone waited with bated breath.

"Aiyee!" Prasert yelped, throwing the bucket of water all over the Abbot. He grabbed another bucket and splashed his wife.

"Wah!" Mook screamed, jumping back, her make-up running down her face. She, too, picked up a bucket and whirled around, drenching everyone in a wide arc. "Whee!"

Now, the Siamese court was bound by rigid protocol. Everything must be done exactly right, according to prescribed rituals and manners. But etiquettes are *brittle*, just like the roof tiles; when they break, they break just as abruptly. In no time at all, the Royal Chancellor, his wife, the chamberlain, guards and retainers all joined the merry bedlam; running around, splashing each other with screams of mirth, slipping and sliding on the wet marble floor, whirling around and sending huge arcs of water in all directions.

Then, as suddenly as it arrived, the storm departed. The sun came out. Everyone was left dripping, empty bucket in hand, looking up at the roof. Thousands of tiny sunbeams shone through holes left by the shattered tiles.

Prasert pointed to Ba, Bo and Bu. The guards grabbed and dragged them before the Royal Chancellor. The 'three rascals' flattened themselves on the floor, trembling and weeping.

"So," the Royal Chancellor glared at them. "So much for your 'golden tiles'."

The Abbot intervened, "Your Excellency, I sense a hidden hand." He turned to gaze upon the Buddha statue, high on the altar. A beam of sunlight shone through a hole, directly on the face. Under this unusual lighting, Buddha's normally serene and impassive face appeared to be… smiling.

"Remember the Middle Path," the Abbot said. 'The path of moderation, nothing in excess. Efficiency, hard work and diligence are all very good… but there are also times when a little fun lights the way to Enlightenment."

Too much fish sauce…

Prasert scowled. He looked upon Buddha's face. Then he looked down at Ba, Bo and Bu, still trembling before him. He sighed deeply, shrugged and said, "Okay. *Mai pen rai…*"

All things considered, the 'three rascals' got off lightly – each was beaten on his buttocks three times with a bamboo stick, had three tufts of hair pulled out and were sent back to the kilns to make new tiles – *but no more durian, saffron or fish sauce!*

Whilst the temple was re-roofed – conventionally – the King heard of the wild goings-on at the aborted consecration. He invited the Abbot to the palace, and before long the rigid protocols of the court dissolved in wet, wild *sanuk*. In fact, the King liked it so much he decreed it an annual festival: *'Songkran'*, the Water Festival.

Mai pen rai: the source of many ills – corruption, inefficiencies, idiotic boo-boos…

Mai pen rai: cure and solace for those ills – gentle tolerance, broadening into a sweet smile…

Is it the biggest curse of the Thai people, or their greatest blessing? Their major weakness or their hidden strength? One can argue this forever, but in the end – well, it doesn't really matter, right?

Mai pen rai.

14 **VIVE LA DIFFERENCE!**

Architectural historians agree the
Chartres Cathedral represents
the apogee of French Gothic
architecture. Yet, it has one
glaring abnormality: whilst
every other cathedral in France
has symmetrical towers on
their west fronts, Chartres
Cathedral's two towers are
obviously mismatched, the
north tower being taller
and more ornate than
the other. How did
this occur?

*The mismatched towers
of Chartres Cathedral.*

The first church on this site burnt down in 858 AD. It was rebuilt and burnt down again in 962 AD; rebuilt and burnt down again in 1020; rebuilt and burnt down again in 1134; rebuilt and burnt down *yet again* in 1160; and finally, in 1194 – it would seem the good people of Chartres had 'arson' written in their DNA.

The fire of 1194 was extensive. Although the bases of the two towers survived, the upper portions collapsed. The townsmen, stirred by the Bishop, went to work at once, rebuilding the choir and nave, and by 1215, this work was well underway.

The Bishop, impatient to see the towers rebuilt, hired *two* master-builders, each with his team of masons. One, headed by Roger de Hauteur, was to build the north tower; the other team, led by William Le Vite, would build the south.

Knowing how architects could dawdle when left to their own devices, the Bishop summoned the two teams after Christmas Mass and announced, "Let there be a competition! A purse of five thousand gold écus, to whichever team that builds the *fastest and tallest!*"

After a slight gleeful pause, the Bishop continued, "Plus, a lifelong dispensation to eat bacon during Lent!"

Thus motivated, both teams made frantic preparations over the winter, but the wily Le Vite stole a march on his rival. Disguising himself as an elderly nun, he snuck into de Hauteur's workshop, and managed to inspect his wooden model. He was pleased to find that de Hauteur had planned a short tower with a single storey and a small spire. Returning to his workshop, Le Vite finalised his design: an octagonal base with eight pointed arches, surmounted by a steeple that would rise at least ten feet higher than de Hauteur's pinnacle.

Spring came, and both teams went to work. Le Vite built rapidly, and by early summer he had completed the octagon and started on his steeple. de Hauteur, by contrast, appeared to be having trouble, for his work proceeded slowly and his piers stopped below the springing of the arches.

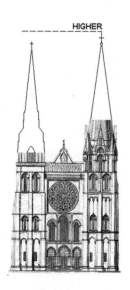

Le Vite was gloating and rubbing his hands, but in fact, he had fallen into a trap.

Knowing Le Vite would spy on him, de Hauteur had built a *deceptively short model*. When he saw Le Vite commencing the base of the steeple – for it would be too late for Le Vite to add another floor – de Hauteur revealed his true intentions. He extended his tower upwards, raising the springing of the arch far higher than what his model showed. This would pump his spire up at least twenty feet, higher than Le Vite's steeple.

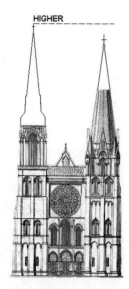

Le Vite was enraged, but not for long. Since he could not add another floor, Le Vite demolished his half-built steeple and rebuilt it at a steeper angle – a steeper steeple. By the end of summer, Le Vite's tower was complete, and its tip would surely soar higher than de Hauteur's pathetic little spire. And Le Vite resumed his gloating.

But his smugness was dispelled when de Hauteur unveiled his second surprise. Having completed his tall floor, *he added yet another floor to his tower.* Of course, this pushed his spire up higher still – an aspiring spire that trumped Le Vite's steeper steeple.

Le Vite was not beaten. He sent his men to Le Havre, purchased a mast from an old ship and smuggled it into his steeple at night. When he saw de Hauteur's spire nearing completion, he cut a hole through the tip of his steeple and pushed the mast through it – adding a crossbar as it went up – and triumphantly erected a crucifix three feet higher than de Hauteur's spire. To be sure, it was an oddly proportioned cross, suitable for a Jesus with short arms and very long legs. But taller was taller.

Furious, de Hauteur disputed Le Vite's action, "Your spire had already been completed! You are not allowed to add more!"

Le Vite merely laughed in de Hauteur's face.

HIGHER

Alas, a storm two days later broke Le Vite's old mast in two. Triumphant, de Hauteur and his team went to the Bishop to claim their reward. The Bishop was now in a quandary, for he did not have the money. The nave had cost more than expected, and he had recently splurged on a lavish row of gargoyles; he had only twenty écus left in the kitty.

As de Hauteur made his claim against a now squirmy Bishop, Le Vite unexpectedly stepped forward to dispute de Hauteur's claim.

de Hauteur glared at him haughtily. "Do you deny that my tower is taller than yours?"

"I agree your tower is taller," Le Vite replied smoothly. "But mine was completed *earlier*."

de Hauteur went pale. "The reward goes to whoever built the *taller*," he gasped.

"No," Le Vite replied. "It goes to whoever built it *faster*."

"Your absurd crucifix broke just last week!"

"The cross was a mere afterthought. My spire was already complete. *You said so yourself.*"

"The prize belongs to the tallest!" de Hauteur screamed.

"The prize belongs to the fastest!" Le Vite yelled.

The clerk consulted his record, "You're *both* right. His Grace promised the prize to whichever team that built *fastest and tallest.*"

Whilst the two architects tried to strangle each other, the Bishop had a brain wave. Pulling the two disputants apart, he said to de Hauteur, "I regret to tell you that you lost, for his steeple was indeed completed first." But before Le Vite could start celebrating, the Bishop turned and said to him, "But you also lost, for his tower is indeed taller than yours."

Whilst the two men gaped at him, the Bishop continued loftily, "You *both* lost. No prize to *either* loser."

If the Bishop thought he could renege on his promise and save himself a bucket of money, he was sadly mistaken. The masons rioted. The Bishop was driven into his palace whilst the builders – now united by a common grievance – stormed into the Cathedral and barricaded themselves inside. They announced that *both* teams had won, and *each team* must be paid the promised prize money. Otherwise, they would set the church on fire.

The Bishop, trying to avoid his liabilities, had ended up doubling it. He appealed to neighbouring lords, but they sneered. In desperation, he imposed a huge tax on the population of Chartres.

For the people of Chartres, this was the last straw. In the past year, they watched, horrified, as their beloved Cathedral sprouted two unequal and mismatched towers; they had seen their Bishop make a mess; and now, they were forced to cough up *double* the prize money…

The good people of Chartres had enough.

The Bishop's residence was set on fire, with the hapless Bishop inside. The angry townsmen then battered down the Cathedral doors and slaughtered all the masons; but reserved different fates for the two chief masons. The first to go was William Le Vite – beheaded in the town square. Then, Roger de Hauteur was hanged, high up in his tower.

"He who finished first, goes first. He who built higher, hangs higher," the rabble muttered.

The King sent a party of armed knights to restore order. The knights arrived to find the town eerily calm, everybody in the Cathedral tearfully attending the funeral of the Bishop. Puzzled, the knights questioned a few men near the door.

"Riot? What riot? Alors, you must have heard wrong! There was no riot."

"*The bishop? Alas, a bolt of lightning struck his house, and he sizzled up, like a rasher of bacon during Lent. Alas! Alas!*"

"*The masons? Oh, they went away. You know architects, a bunch of fly-by-nights.*"

"*The mismatched towers? Oh, but don't you just love them? They're… so cute! So different!*"

"*Vive la différence!*"

15 **INVERTED CATHEDRAL**

Medieval cathedrals usually took a long time to complete, often centuries. Work would start and then stop, as towns run out of funds and needed time to gather more. Thus, it is normal for a cathedral to exhibit a variety of styles in sequence – for instance, Romanesque at the bottom, Early Gothic in the middle, Late Gothic at the towers, and so on.

The cathedral of Guten-Baden also exhibited this mélange of styles – but puzzlingly, in *reverse* order. The base was Florentine Renaissance. Above it was late French Gothic, with pointed arches and rows of statues. Further up, we find early Gothic, and the towers were Romanesque, stark and boxy with rounded arches. In short, the cathedral looked as though it had been built *from top-down.* Stylistically and chronologically, the cathedral of Guten-Baden was upside down.

This puzzling cathedral was first noticed by Eugene Viollet-le-Duc, the French architectural historian who passed through Guten-Baden in 1862. He never saw anything like it.

The 'Inverted Cathedral' of Guten-Baden, circa 1903.

Returning three months later, he tried to research its history – and promptly discovered there was none.

Guten-Baden had the misfortune to stand at the boundaries of the Catholic and Protestant states during the Thirty Years' War (1618 - 1648). It was captured by the Protestant army in 1622, resulting in massacre and much damage. In 1625, Spanish forces recaptured the city, burnt several thousand 'heretics' in a huge *auto-da-fe* and started a fire that destroyed half the town hall, including the archives. Six years later, the Protestants, under Gustavus Adolphus, returned and history repeated itself; the town hall was flattened, and the last traces of the archive were destroyed. The city changed hands so many times and suffered so much destruction, that by the time of the Treaty of Westphalia (which ended the war in 1648) it was deserted, and settlers had to be lured from other parts of Germany to repopulate it.

In short, there was no written history, and no oral tradition. No clues at all about how the cathedral was built, not even when the construction started. Frustrated, Viollet-le-Duc sent appeals to surrounding towns, but the result was paltry and uninformative. Stumped, he published his observations in a book, *The Good and Bad of Guten-Baden*, challenging the readers to propose an explanation. This was a start of the 'Guten-Baden Mystery' that would engage the attention of European architects for the next half-century.

Eventually, Viollet-le-Duc himself came up with an explanation, which he published in 1865:

"The entire building was erected at one phase, around the tenth century, and in the Romanesque style. But by the thirteenth century the Romanesque was outmoded, and the locals decided to recase the structure in the more fashionable Gothic. They hacked off the Romanesque decoration, added a fresh layer of stone, and proceeded to carve it in the Gothic style. However, they must have run out of money, for the recasing stopped at the base of the tower. Then, during the fifteenth century, they attempted to recase the structure again, this time in the Rayonnant style but gave up at an even lower level. The last attempt was during the Renaissance, most probably by a mason trained in Florence, but it never got further than the bottom storey. How like the Germans to start something and not see it through!"

This explanation was accepted by most historians, except the Germans – no doubt incensed by Viollet-le-Duc's parting shot. In fact, young Friedrich Nietzsche was so annoyed he spent three months investigating the cathedral, and even persuaded the Bishop to let him drill for samples at various parts of the cathedral's walls. And the result, announced in 1868, were conclusive and stunning:

"The core samples show no sign whatsoever of a later cladding. The carvings were integral. In other words, stones were stacked up to form the building and the carvings were cut directly into the surface. There was no later addition. How like the French, lacking the Will to Power, to think in terms of wrapping things up, like putting on a pretty-pretty dress and pom-poms to hide their lack of substance."

Viollet-le-Duc retaliated by calling Nietzsche a 'Sauerkraut-head' and the latter branded Viollet-le-Duc 'The French Dressmaker'. Angry books, articles and pamphlets were published, resulting in the Franco-Prussian War of 1870. In 1876, the English joined the fray when John Ruskin, an art critic, speculated:

"The entire cathedral was built all at once, but in the rough, without any decoration whatsoever. The carving then proceeded from the top-down. The masons carved the top bit in the Norman style (or, as you chaps on the continent would call it, the Romanesque). Then, for some reason, they came to a halt. The carving resumed several centuries later, so they did it in the Gothic style. That would be the bit in the middle. Then, work stopped again. Bit by bit they proceeded downwards, adopting whatever was the current style, until they finished at the bottom, ending in a sort of Florentine base. It may seem an odd way of building a cathedral, but it did have the advantage that falling chips and debris could not possibly damage any work previously done below, because there was none."

Unfortunately, this explanation failed to make peace. Nietzsche sneered, "Typical inverted British logic." Ruskin pointed out that Nietzsche was not an architect; Nietzsche replied that neither was Ruskin. Ruskin then challenged Nietzsche to come up with an explanation, but the latter could only splutter, "The superman obeys no rules; with the Will to Power, he may flout all convention, and build any way he pleases." In 1886, Ruskin rebutted him in an article entitled '*Thus Spake Jabberwocky*'.

A more serious objection to Ruskin's theory was that there was no example of any other building ever built in such a manner. Besides, medieval masons were quite competent in protecting the completed work below from falling debris. And so, the 'Guten-Baden Mystery' remained unsolved, as stubborn and recalcitrant as the 'Man in the Iron Mask'. Eventually public interest died, and the cathedral, largely forgotten, slumbered through World War I.

But, the Second World War was a different matter. By then, Guten-Baden had become a significant industrial centre, with a large ball bearing factory on its outskirts. Since ball bearings were used in many weapons, the Allied powers considered it a military target, and in the winter of 1943, Eisenhower ordered the factory bombed. On 12 November that year, five B-29 Super Fortresses, escorted by fighters, took off from their base in England. After struggling past an attempted blockade by the Luftwaffe and heavy fire from the ground, they trained their state-of-the-art bombsight over the target. After two hours of intensive and relentless precision-bombing, they succeeded in completely flattening… *the cathedral.*

Upon returning to base, the bomber crew could only go – "oops…".

Churchill kept silent in public, but in his private diary he recorded: "How a group of highly-trained airmen could possibly mistake a tall, spiky cathedral for a flat, sprawling factory twenty miles away, is beyond the ability of reason to explain… except that the crew had been making bathtub

The cathedral, after too much Kickapoo Joy Juice.

gin again, along with Kickapoo Joy Juice, in the privacy of
their quarters."

In defence of the aircrew, Eisenhower announced,
"Everyone makes mistakes. But it takes a ***helluvalot*** of guts
to fly through dangerous airspace, fight the Luftwaffe and
make it through to the ball bearing factory! Even though they
bombed the wrong place, it took balls, man!"

General Charles de Gaulle whispered to his aide, "*Les
Americains*, they got balls, but no bearing."

After the war, the rubble was removed to a nearby lake and
used as landfill. A new satellite town, Guten-Nauff, was
constructed over it. Yet even when pulverised and buried, the
cathedral continued to stir up debate.

In the seventies, Erik Von Dinkum claimed that the cathedral was indeed built from top-down, but with the help of aliens: a flying saucer, using its anti-gravity force field, *held* the towers in mid-air whilst the lower portions were added. Science-fiction writer Isaac Asimovie proposed (possibly tongue-in-cheek) that *time moved backwards* in Guten-Baden: "Of course, they built it from the bottom-up. Starting in the fifteenth century, they built in the Renaissance style. Then later, around the thirteenth century, they added a Gothic upper section. By the tenth century, they completed the towers in Romanesque style. Too bad they stopped. Otherwise, we'd see a Greek temple on top!"

By the time The Society of Witches and People for Pyramid Power started making claims, German Chancellor Willy Brandt decided that leaving the cathedral buried under Guten-Nauff was not good enough, and proposed the landfill be dug up and the fragments be reassembled, to determine the truth once and for all. The proposal was held up for years due to the cost of resettling the entire town – and finally scuttled by the 2008 financial meltdown.

So, the mystery of the Inverted Cathedral of Guten-Baden remains unsolved, deeply buried in a lake… until such time someone can explain how a perfectly normal catherdral can be built upside-down.

16 TELESCOPIC TEMPLE

The Temple of Prayer – the most important building in the Temple of Heaven complex in Beijing – is a circular hall with three tiers of roofs, standing on three tiers of marble platforms. It is visited by millions of tourists every year, but most would be very surprised to know that this calm and serene building was once much, *much* taller, but managed, incredibly, to *telescope* itself into its present shape.

The Temple of Prayer today – in its shrunken form.

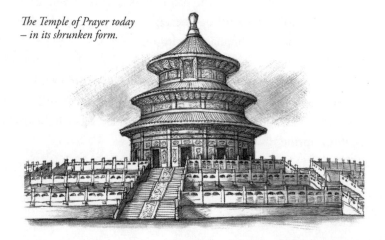

Fed up with the hot, muggy summers of Nanjing, Yongle, the third Emperor of the Ming Dynasty, moved his capital to Beijing. (For readers unfamiliar with *Pinyin*, Yongle is pronounced '*yong ler*'; it does not rhyme with 'bongle', although it would be fun to do so, since he is dead.) In 1406, he commenced the building of the Forbidden City, and around the same time he also started the construction of the Temple of Heaven. For the latter, the Chief Carpenter designed a round building with three tiers of roof – exactly what we see today – and it was approved by the Emperor.

For such an important building, the Chief Carpenter ordered tropical hardwood from Burma. It took six months for the hardwood to arrive overland, and so hard and strong was the wood that the cutting and carving wore out many sets of tools. After four months of intensive work, the columns and beams were brought to the triple-tiered marble platform and erected, without nails, using only mortise-and-tenon joints. Only tiling and painting remained, but unfortunately, it was at this moment the Emperor chose to inspect the work.

In Chinese, Yongle means 'always happy' but the Emperor was not happy just then. "I don't like it," he said to the Chief Carpenter. "Too squat, it looks like a mushroom. It should be taller. Why not *add* another floor, just squeeze it in between the first and second levels. That should do it."

The Chief Carpenter gasped.

The Chief Minister whispered to the Emperor. "Your Majesty, four is not a good number… it sounds like the word 'death'."

Yongle frowned. "Superstition! But all the same, to keep you happy, how about *five* floors? It symbolises the Five Elements – Water, Earth, Metal, Fire and uh… Wine, if I recall correctly."

"Your Majesty," the Chief Carpenter implored. "We have used up all the Burmese hardwood. There is only a little left, not enough for two new floors! It would take us another six months to get more. Think of the delay! We cannot possibly get it completed by the New Year!"

"Rubbish!" the Emperor exploded. "You builders are all the same, always wanting the most expensive materials! Are you waiting for Admiral Zhenghe to come back with a load of Burmese teak? Local wood is good enough. Use Fragrant Pine, I like the smell. It will make the endless chanting more bearable."

He glared at the Chief Carpenter and went away.

The Chief Carpenter had no choice. He dismantled the second and third floors, leaving only the first level intact, and added two extra floors, each floor stepping slightly inwards. Above the newly erected floors, he put back the original second and third floors – now the new fourth and fifth floors. The interpolation was built of Fragrant Pine, as the Emperor wished. Unfortunately, this was a soft wood that introduced a dangerous weakness in the building, and the Chief Carpenter prayed desperately to Guanyin for protection. Perhaps the prayers were effective, for the building was completed in time for the New Year ceremonies.

But right afterwards, the Emperor ordered the Chief Carpenter brought before him.

"I don't like it," he said. "Five is actually not a lucky number. Now *seven* is lucky. Everybody likes it. There are Seven Dragons, Seven Daughters of the Jade Emperor, Seven Levels of Heaven… all good things come in sevens. And of course, the seventh day of the seventh month is when the moon is especially beautiful."

The Chief Carpenter nearly choked. "Your Majesty, this will make it a pagoda, not a hall!"

"Whatever!" the Emperor said airily and departed.

So, the disheartened Chief Carpenter dismantled the top level with its conical roof and added yet another two floors. Since the temple had to be ready by the *next* New Year, again Fragrant Pine was used, thus introducing another weak point. Work was completed by the time the Emperor summoned the Chief Carpenter again.

"I want *one* more floor," demanded Yongle. "Why do you look so pale? Eight is even better than seven. The Eightfold Path of Buddha. The Daoist Octogram. The Eight Immortals! Also *fa-cai*, getting rich."

There was no reply. The Chief Carpenter had fainted.

As it turned out, there was no need for the Chief Carpenter to worry, for Heaven took matters out of his hands. A week later, a violent earthquake shook Beijing. The entire city rocked, but as the Temple of Prayer was the tallest structure, it suffered the worst, with its tips swaying back and forth drunkenly.

Left: Computer simulation of the Temple of Prayer as built.
Right: The actual temple today.

To understand what happened next, here is a summary of the building's structure. The first, fourth and seventh levels were made of Burmese hardwood. They were the original three tiers, but now separated from each other by the second and third, and fifth and sixth floors constructed of weak pine wood. Imagine three hard, heavy pebbles with layers of potato chips stuffed in between.

Under earthquake stresses, the Burmese hardwood held up well, but the soft Fragrant Pine splintered and disintegrated. The sixth floor collapsed, followed by the fifth, sending the entire seventh floor crashing downwards – *as one single unit* – on to the fourth floor. The fourth floor shuddered but did not break. Instead, it crushed the weak third and second Fragrant Pine floors. As they collapsed, they sent the fourth floor plunging down to the first floor, still upright, still wearing the seventh floor like a cap.

Within sixty seconds, the hall had *telescoped* itself from seven floors down to the original three. Even more incredibly, it was still standing – slightly twisted and leaning at an angle, all the roof tiles scattered and its interior chock full of pine splinters – but amazingly, still standing.

Yongle - who had been toying around with the idea of having *nine* floors – had to admit defeat. Quoting General Cao-Cao, he philosophically mused: "The calculations of man can't beat the calculations of Heaven."

It took the Chief Carpenter a month to dismantle everything and clear the debris. To his astonishment, most of the hardwood columns and beams were still useable; only a few needed replacing. The temple was reassembled, but along original lines: *three* levels, no more.

Heaven had spoken, enough was enough.

Several centuries later, Vice-Premier Zhou Enlai was told the story. He grimaced and said, "I've heard of building contractors, but never a building contract-*ing*!"

17 GIVE FACE

According to Florentine legend, Minias was a Roman general who secretly converted to Christianity. When Emperor Decius found out, Minias was thrown to the panthers. However, the panthers refused to devour him. "Christians are so bitter. Can't they give us some Zoroastrians instead?"

The Emperor ordered Minias beheaded, whereupon the saint picked up his head, tucked it under his arms, crossed River Arno and climbed a hill outside Florence, where he invented bowling.

Around the eleventh century, a monasterial church was erected on the hilltop – San Miniato al Monte, dedicated to Minias, the first Christian martyr of Florence. But Florentinos have one habit: they never finish

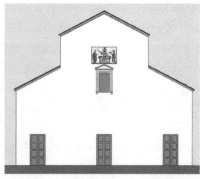

San Miniato al Monte.

anything. "Why do today what you can do tomorrow?" they often said. "We must leave something for the next generation!" As a result, the west fronts of Florentine churches – the main entrances – were often left blank. So too, was San Miniato al Monte's.

Churches raised funds by building side chapels which they would sell to noble families as private chapels. The family could worship and be buried there – like owning a penthouse on Fifth Avenue, only closer to God. But the little church of San Miniato al Monte was out of town, and on top of a tall hill. Although it offered a great panorama of Florence, it was troublesome to get to. No family wanted a chapel there – it would be like owning a penthouse in the Bronx (or worse, Queens). Only Pozzo Il Pazzi, the founder of the Pazzi clan, was buried there, because he wanted to be away from his relatives.

With little resources, the Abbot struggled to put on a brave face to the world. He scrounged two old pillars from Santa Reparata (demolished to make way for the Duomo) and used that to erect a frame around the central window, with a little pediment. Above that he added a small panel

'Christ Doing Something'.

of mosaic, showing '*Christ Doing Something*', with the gold background typical of the Byzantine style. This was expensive and he could afford only a small patch.

The Middle Ages waned, and the Renaissance kicked in. One by one, the major churches received their facades. Leon Battista Alberti designed a facade for the Santa Maria Novella (so-called because it was new, not because the contents were fictitious). Alberti was a polymath Renaissance Man – author, artist, architect, poet, linguist, philosopher, cryptographer and mahjong champion. His design, using white, green and pink marble proved a triumph, especially the skillful way he surrounded the circular window with mahjong tiles. It was perfection: "Nothing can be added, nor taken away, without marring the whole."

Mahjong tiles on Santa Maria Novella, by Alberti.

After the facade was unveiled, Lorenzo de' Medici – known as 'Lorenzo the Magnificent' – brought Alberti to San Miniato al Monte. Alberti, who had been hoping for a major commission, stared at the little church with some disappointment.

"Okay, I know this isn't the St. Peter's," Lorenzo growled. "But I promised to sponsor a new facade for this little church. It's a peace offering to the Pazzi family – their ancestor Pozzo is buried inside."

"Peace offering? Why, Sire, have you offended them?"

Lorenzo reddened. "Well… Just the other day, I met Francesco de' Pazzi in the streets but called him 'Signor *Pizza*', by mistake…"

Alberti doubled-up with laughter, "Well, his face *is* rather round and splotchy."

"That wasn't the reason!" Lorenzo cried. "At least, not consciously. Don't tell anyone, but I'm… dyslexic. I tend to mix up the letters 'A' and 'I'…"

Alberti chuckled, "So you better butter them up before they kill you, right?"

He returned his gaze to the church, "The three doors at ground level are okay, but the square window and that little patch of mosaic in the middle will have to go. I want to cut a big round window where they are…"

"No!" Lorenzo objected. "You can block up the window, but that mosaic stays. It is miraculous."

"Miraculous? How so?"

"Ten years ago, Sister Adilla – our Sunday School teacher – came trudging up these stairs. Nobody knows why she came, because when she reached the top, she stared up at the mosaic – gasped, and dropped dead."

"Sire, you call *that* a miracle?"

"It was a miracle," Lorenzo said, firmly. "She was a horrid old harridan. She used to catch us at our catechisms and whack us with a metal ruler whenever we get a single word wrong. Her idea of personal adornment was a noose. We used to call her 'Adilla the Nun' – behind her back, of course. Every year, the Signoria leads a solemn procession up here... to give thanks to the mosaic."

Adilla the Nun. (Note the noose under her skirt.)

"But the mosaic is in the way! I want my big round window!" Alberti whined.

"Sorry, but even geniuses must design around limitations... Look, you're supposed to be the polymath – so poly it!"

Grumbling, Alberti measured the walls and started to design a facade. As he foresaw, the three doors were easy; a blind arcade of five arches unified them neatly, but the nave was more difficult, because its roof was higher than those on the

First facade design, San Miniato al Monte.

aisles. Alberti chopped off the side roofs as little triangles, and briefly contemplated putting *Birth of Venus* in them, but decided that would not go down well with the Abbot. He then filled the central window and designed a giant circle around the mosaic.

However, the Abbot objected to losing the window.

"Lorenzo said I can block it up!" Alberti whined.

"Do you know how dark it is inside?" the Abbot snapped.

"But the circle is the perfect form and the mosaic fits beautifully into the centre…"

The Abbot peered at the drawing. "Looks more like an archery target with Jesus Christ smacked in the middle. We are taught to aim for Heaven but not quite *that* literally!"

In his next attempt, Alberti replicated the Novella format – no longer novel, but even geniuses must recycle. This involved

Second facade design, San Miniato al Monte.

enlarging the central window to a big round one, but the mason objected.

"I can't cut such a large window so close to the mosaic. There's not enough wall left to support it – it will collapse!"

"Then what size window *can* I have?" Alberti asked in exasperation.

The mason sketched a window, about one third the size of Alberti's.

"Damn that nun!" Alberti hissed. "Why couldn't she drop dead looking at something else?"

One day, Alberti got a brain wave. "If you can't lick 'em, join 'em," said Alberti the tactician. In this next design, he *expanded* the mosaic sideways by triplicating it, until it stretched right across the nave. On the two spaces below, he placed two circles. Proudly, he showed the result to the Abbot.

Third facade design, San Miniato al Monte.

"*Three* Jesus Christs?" the Abbot asked, incredulously.

"Father, Son and the Holy Ghost," said Alberti, the theologian.

The Abbot peered at the drawing and shook his head. "The Holy Spirit is usually shown as a dove – and placed between the Father and Son, sort of glues them together."

"That's easy, we'll just replace the panel in the middle with a big white dove."

"What? You will destroy the miraculous mosaic!"

"But you have another two just like it!" Alberti pleaded. "Twice as miraculous!"

"Miracles don't work that way," the Abbot snarled, and went away.

In the end, Alberti gave up. He divided the rectangle into three vertical panels, thus isolating the mosaic and the window in the middle panel. On the left and right panels,

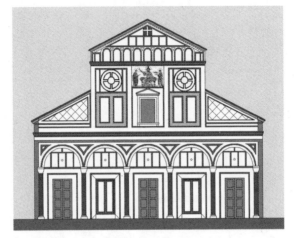

Final facade design, San Miniato al Monte.

he inserted a circle, each with a little round window in the middle, added some rectangles underneath, and called it a day.

"Perfection is when nothing can be added, nor taken away," he muttered. "Well, I can't add anything more, and can't take away that damn mosaic, so it is as close to perfection as I will ever get…"

He handed the drawing to Michelozzo Michelozzi, the architect who was to execute the work.

"Say, how did you get such a funny name?" Alberti asked, curiously.

Michelozzo Michelozzi grinned. "When I was born, my folks consulted a Gypsy fortune-teller, and she said I will grow up to be an architect," he said. "So they gave me a symmetrical name, because, architects love symmetry."

"More like your parents are dyslexic and got their 'I' and 'O' confused," Alberti muttered.

Alberti returned to Rimini for the winter, where he worked for the ruling family, whose name 'Malatesta' literally meant 'bad head'. At spring the following year, he received word from Michelozzi that the new cladding was completed; the scaffolds would be removed shortly, and the facade would be visible in its entirety.

Alberti hurried back to Florence, went straight up the hill, impatient to see the result. On the way he encountered large crowds, some going up, others coming down. It seemed that *tout Firenze* have turned out to see the new facade. Oddly, those coming down either grinned at Alberti, or scowled ferociously at him. He could not understand why.

At the top of the stairs were Lorenzo and his wife, Clarice Orsini. Lorenzo was screaming and tearing his hair. As soon as he saw Alberti, he grabbed him by the throat, trying to throttle him.

"What have you done?!" he cried. "What kind of a joke is this?"

Alberti stared in bewilderment. "Sire? What are you talking about?"

"Look at it! Is this your idea of a stupid joke?" Lorenzo yelled, pointing at the facade.

Alberti looked up at his new facade. Michelozzi had followed his drawing exactly. There was nothing wrong.

"Sire, what is the matter?" he stammered.

"Are you trying to get me killed?" Lorenzo screamed, white-faced.

"Well, *I* like it," his wife Clarice piped up unexpectedly.

Alberti bowed to her politely, but still confused.

"A pity you hadn't given him a neck, Signor Alberti," she said.

Alberti stared at her, befuddled. *Him? Neck?*

"He looks kind of hunched," Clarice added, helpfully.

Alberti turned and looked again at his facade, and then – *HE SAW IT.*

Suddenly he understood why Lorenzo was so frantic, and why everyone he met either laughed or growled at him. Had

Surprise!

he not been so preoccupied with the geometry, he would have seen it sooner, too…

What he had put on the facade of San Miniato al Monte was a *FACE*.

The two circles were eyes, wide-open, with the round windows being the pupils. The old window in between looked like a little mouth, gaping open. The pediment over the window looked like a snub nose. As for the mosaic – that blasted mosaic that caused all the trouble – it resembled a patch of gold foil glued on the bridge of the nose. It was a face – eyes popping and mouth agape in surprise.

Alberti was not a polymath for nothing, and one of his less-advertised professions was a Fluent Liar. He thought rapidly and bowed to Lorenzo.

"Sire, I have done what you asked. I had given the church a new facade."

"Facade? You call *that* a facade? A stupid face?"

"Sire, those words are cognates. Face, facing, facility, facade… They all derive from the same root," replied Alberti the etymologist. "Moreover, since the saint had been beheaded, I had given him a new head, and a face to go with it. Is it not appropriate?"

"He looks just like my pet Pekinese, Mimi," Clarice added delightedly. "Can we rename this church San Mimi-alto?"

"The Pazzi clan will *kill* me!" Lorenzo wailed. "They'll think I did it deliberately! They'll be so insulted! They will lose face!"

"How can they lose face if you gave them a face?" Asked Alberti, looking puzzled.

"Well, give them *something else*," said Clarice. "Say, a family chapel, in that miserable little church, Santa Croce. Their very own Pazzi Chapel! It can be designed by that foul-tempered little mason… What's his name… Filippo Brunelleschi, if I recall correctly."

Lorenzo glared, and without a word stomped down the stairs, black fumes emanating from his head.

Alberti went back to Rimini, and swore never to set foot in Florence again. "'Malatesta' may mean 'bad head' but at least that's better than 'no head'," he said, philosophically.

Very true, for on 26 April 1478, the Pazzi clan *did* attempt to kill Lorenzo in church; but being muddled, they killed the wrong man instead.

Decades later, the Signoria debated about changing the facade of San Miniato al Monte. At length the idea was dropped when Girolamo Savonarola, the mad monk, proposed to burn the entire church down, as a Bonfire of the Vanities. The Signoria arrested him and burnt *him* at his very own bonfire instead.

And so, San Miniato al Monte remained unchanged, as Alberti left it – a rather cute face with an astonished expression, gazing over the rooftops of Florence. But then, if you had been headless for a thousand years, and suddenly somebody gave you a new face, wouldn't you look surprised too?

18 LOOKING FOR FLAWS

Rarely does architecture have an impact on the fate of empires. But who would have thought, that tiny errors made in the interior decor could bring down an entire dynasty and change the course of history?

The Alhambra was originally built as a fortress by the Moorish kings of Granada, Spain, and its exterior, even today, still retained a forbidding appearance. But from the twelfth century onwards, successive rulers of the Nasrid dynasty transformed the interior of the Alhambra into a wonderland of decorative carving and stucco work; their motto being 'cover every square inch and then some more'. The most dazzling creations were the incredibly facetted vaults over the Hall of the Abencerrajes, and the Hall of the Two Sisters.

The Caliphate of Cordoba – of which Granada was part – had set itself up as a rival to the Caliphate of Baghdad, and the artisans of Alhambra remained true to Persian traditions: they included a deliberate mistake in each vault, since perfection was for God alone. Theologically correct, but unfortunately,

There was a deliberate mistake made in this ceiling. Can you find it?

they never told anyone just exactly *where* the flaws were. This triggered a tragic sequence of events that resulted in the fall of Granada.

By the fifteenth century, a resurgent Catholic expansion had whittled away most of the Moorish kingdom, and Granada became the last Islamic outpost on the Iberian Peninsula. In 1482, Abu 'Abdallah Muhammad XII became the Sultan of the Emirate of Granada. The Spanish mangled it to 'Boabdil'. To revenge the insult, Boabdil invaded Castile, but was taken prisoner in 1484. He was freed in 1487 after he agreed to hold Granada as a tributary kingdom under the Catholic monarchs and retired to Alhambra to enjoy its beauty and pleasures.

It was then that somebody – most unwisely – told him about the deliberate flaws in the vaults. At first the information seemed to have no effect. But a month later, he summoned his ministers to the Hall of Abencerrajes.

Now, this hall had a dark history, despite its gorgeous ceiling. According to legend, a previous sultan feared the power of the Abencerrajes clan, so he invited all their men to dinner – and slaughtered them as they entered the hall, leaving a dark red stain in the fountain that could not be removed. (Modern executives please take note: this is *not* an approved way to cut back on entertainment expenses.)

So, when the ministers arrived at the hall, they were disconcerted to find Boabdil lying on the floor, resembling one of the victims in the legend – except his eyes were open and staring at the ceiling. They prostrated, as etiquette demanded, but it was hard to prostrate to a man already flat on his back.

"Your Majesty… Are you ill?" a minister enquired anxiously.

"I can't find it," Boabdil said, after a long silence.

The ministers looked at each other.

"The flaw," Boabdil said, fretfully. "I can't find the flaw."

The ministers were obliged to lie on their backs as well –

painfully, as they were elderly and arthritic – and squinted up at the ceiling, attempting to spot the deliberate flaw. They failed, and were obliged to stop when the sun set, and oil lamps proved too dim to illuminate the ceiling adequately.

It was repeated the next morning.

This became a regular ritual, with Boabdil lying around the Hall of Abencerrajes in different positions, accompanied by his ministers, all gazing up at the ceiling until their eyes smarted. State affairs were transacted thus:

"Your Majesty, the Catholics are getting aggressive again," his Chief Minister would say from the south west corner of the hall, trying to sound stern, although it was difficult to sound stern whilst flat on his back.

"Yes, yes… Help me find the flaw," the Sultan – also on his back – would reply.

"Your Majesty, we must recruit more soldiers!"

"Do you think that yellowish bit over there is the flaw? Or just a stain?"

After a while, Boabdil dismissed his ministers and called in young men from the kitchen, stables and town. "Your eyes are young. A purse of gold to whoever finds the flaw!"

Thus, the Hall of Abencerrajes was filled with young men lying all over the floor in various strange positions. The ministers, left outside, peeked in through the half-closed door.

"What's going on?" the Chief Minister whispered to his colleague.

"Maybe our Sultan had just slaughtered another clan?"

"I don't see any blood."

"Or maybe he got bored with his harem and decided to try an orgy with men… Look at that one, he's got his head propped on another man's tummy!"

"Nah! He's just using him as a pillow."

"But look! He's opening his mouth and turning his head toward the other man's… Eek!"

"Don't be silly, he's just yawning. Not what I would call sodomy. Besides, they are all looking up, not at each other."

"I get it. They are all searching for the blasted flaw in the ceiling!"

"Oh, *that* again. Frankly, it would be better if they just sodomised each other," the Chief Minister grumbled. "At least it would be over and done with!"

Secretly, the ministers bribed some of the young men to 'find' the flaws, but Boabdil was not so easily fooled.

"Your Majesty! I found the flaw! It's over there!" a young man would cry from time to time.

"Where?" the Sultan would crawl over and stare.

"There! That dark bit next to the third facet on the fifth tier, second from the right…"

The Sultan would gaze and then say, "Nah…That's just a shadow. Look again!"

After three months of failure, Boabdil went over to the Hall of the Two Sisters. This hall had a facetted ceiling every bit as complex as the other.

"I can't find the flaw in the Hall of Abencerrajes," he told the Sultana and his mother disconsolately. "You help me look here. Maybe we'll have better luck in this room."

The Hall of the Two Sisters soon became the Hall of Too Many Sisters, as the entire harem – along with any children old enough – laid themselves out on the floor, eyes searching. This started to look like a heterosexual orgy, except the ladies were all in a terrible temper.

"Your Majesty… Was *this* what you married me for?" his Sultana asked plaintively.

"Shut up... Lying flat on your back is part of your job."

"On a soft bed, Sire, *not* on cold hard marble!"

"Get yourself a cushion if you want, just search for the flaw!" Boabdil snapped.

"Why is it so important?" his mother – who refused to participate – demanded.

"It's driving me crazy," the Sultan sobbed. "There must be a flaw somewhere, if I can only find it!"

Failing to find the flaw, the Sultan returned his attention to the Hall of the Abencerrajes, where he built a wooden scaffold, so he could climb up and examine the ceiling closely. This did not help much since he could no longer see the entire design. As an aid, he hired artists who would painstakingly copy a typical segment of the dome, from base to the tip, and use that to compare against every other segment. Three artists went blind in the process, and one went mad.

His Chief Minister interrupted one day. "Your Majesty, Queen Isabella has sent in an ultimatum."

"What does the silly bitch want?"

"She wants you to surrender Granada."

"Why? Does she want to search for the flaws too?"

Boabdil ordered another scaffold to be built in the Hall of the Two Sisters. As this was in the women's quarters and it was unthinkable that the women be seen by outsiders, they were forbidden to enter the hall whilst the scaffold was being built, resulting in traffic confusion. When the scaffold was completed, the hall was reopened to the women – who knew, with a sinking feeling, just what was demanded of them. At least the scaffolds were upholstered.

Whilst lying on their backs one day, searching the ceiling they had come to hate, the ladies heard a great noise from outside. Boabdil, off in one corner examining a particularly convoluted facet, heard it too. He summoned the Chief Minister.

"Your Majesty, we are under attack," his Chief Minister replied gloomily.

"Who dares to attack us?" the Sultan demanded.

"King Ferdinand."

Boabdil thought for a moment, and asked, "Who's he?"

The Chief Minister was struck speechless. "Your Majesty! He is the husband of Queen Isabella! Have you forgotten?"

"Oh yes... That's what you get when two rulers marry each other. They come in pairs, like matching bookends." Suddenly, he was struck by a terrible thought and blurted: "*This is the Hall of Two Sisters. Suppose* the *craftsmen left two deliberate defects? I'll never find both!*"

Giving up in despair, the Chief Minister opened the city gates and surrendered to the Catholic forces.

There might be TWO deliberate mistakes in this ceiling!

As Boabdil and his retainers rode away into exile, he paused on the crest of a hill to take one last, tearful look at the Alhambra. His mother told him contemptuously, "Thou dost weep like a woman for what thou could not defend as a man." (Mothers are *so* loving and caring.)

Boabdil went into exile in Morocco, but the flaws that eluded him troubled him for the rest of his life. Even on his deathbed, he fretted. The Imam arrived to hear him muttering to himself, "Where are they? I know they are there! I know those ceilings like the back of my hand! I had examined every facet, every corner, every single crook and nanny – I mean, nook and cranny! Yet I could not detect a single flaw, not one! Where did I go wrong?"

"Perhaps Allah is teaching you something," the Imam said gently.

"What could that be?"

"The biggest flaw of them all… is *looking* for flaws..." the Imam replied.

A strange light came into Boabdil's eyes; then a tremulous smile spread over his lips, as he finally, finally, understood.

"Thank you," he said, and died.

19 A SENSE OF PROPORTION

The Philippines is full of churches, but probably the strangest one is the San Agustin Church in the town of Paoay, in northern Luzon. If you approach the church from the front, the first thing you notice is how squat it is. Most churches aspire to be as tall as possible, but the Paoay church hugs close to the ground, short and fat. Instead of soaring to Heaven, it looks more like a hedgehog diving into its burrow.

Hedgehog diving into its burrow.

But as you walk to the side of the Church, the next oddity comes in sight: a row of incredibly huge buttresses, each one as thick as a room. Hong Kong visitors invariably sigh, wishing they had apartments as big. Indeed, these buttresses look like they were designed to withstand an atomic bomb, rather than just hold up the sides of a building.

Architectural historians say this is an example of 'Spanish Colonial Earthquake Baroque' designed to withstand frequent earthquakes. Yet the reasoning seems strange, for the *front* facade has no buttressing; its shallow little pilasters are purely decorative and will be of no use at all in a tremblor. What's the point of the sides surviving, if the front wall falls flat on its face?

Ready for nuclear attack!

And finally, when you enter the church, the third oddity becomes apparent: the church is inordinately long, compared to its width. It is more like a tunnel than a hall. At 110 metres (360 feet) it can be used as a rifle range. If filled to capacity, those at the last pew will need telescopes to see the altar. Paoay's population in 2015 was just 24,866, and probably less at the time it was built; so why did the diocese need the church to be so long? And if it did need the space, why not build transepts, the usual solution?

The sad truth was, its builders did not trust their senses – if they had any.

In 1551, missionary Francis Xavier made a secret trip to the Philippines. His mission was to set up a Jesuit seminary to train priests, for a planned effort to land in southern China. He ignored the bright lights of Manila (too many distractions) and chose a spot on the west coast of North Luzon – as close to China as he could get, and isolated enough that the young seminarians would not chase after women or little boys. That spot chosen was Paoay.

Converting the locals posed few difficulties, but getting them to accept dogma was another matter, especially Transubstantiation. The Catholic Church held that during Communion, the bread and wine *literally* turned into the flesh and blood of Christ – somehow, miraculously, the carbohydrates turned into human protein and the ethyl alcohol turned into human blood corpuscles.

The locals were puzzled, "But Father, they *taste* like bread and wine."

"You cannot trust your senses, they deceive you!" Xavier sternly told them. "You must have Faith and believe!"

"You mean, it *really* turns into flesh and blood?"

"Yes."

"Eek! We are not cannibals! If you want cannibals, go to Mindanao!"

Giving up on a fruitless argument, Xavier turned to the bigger problem of setting up a seminary and a church. The seminary was easy; he hired local carpenters to put up some huts – missionaries were expected to live rough. But the church was another matter; it must be grand and beautiful, not only as homage to God but also to impress the congregation.

Xavier wrote to an architect in Manila, Ramos de Casabasta, and gave rough specifications. After three months he got impatient, and sent a friar to chase – everyone knew how architects could dilly-dally. After a fortnight, the friar returned with a doleful look, carrying several rolls of drawings. There was a letter, written in shaky handwriting, from the dying architect.

"To Father Francis,
There's an epidemic. I am dying of yellow fever. Plans nearly complete, hope it will do. My draftsman died before adding dimensions, so you will have to scale off. All drawings are quarter inch to one foot. Am sending all my scale rules, as I shall need them no more. Farewell, adios.
Ramos de Casabasta
P.S. – When I go up there, will I still have to eat and drink Him, or unnecessary?

After saying an *Ave Maria* for de Casabasta, Xavier summoned his assistants, friars Guido and Guillermo, and showed them the drawings. They were very nearly complete. The plan showed a simple rectangular church, 180 feet long; the elevation showed a tall facade in the Gothic style. (This was the early 1500s; the Renaissance had not reached the boonies.)

"There are no dimensions," Brother Guido said. "How do we build it?"

"Ramos said the drawings are 1/4" to 1'-0". In other words, a quarter of an inch on the drawing represents one foot on the ground."

Rummaging amongst the pile of scale rules, he found the appropriate one, and showed it to the two men, "See the markings?"

The two friars looked puzzled.

"I'll show you!" Xavier said. "It's quite simple, really."

He led them to the site, already flattened and cleared. He laid the plan on the ground and used the scale rule to measure the width of the nave. Inserting a peg in the soil, he used a measuring rod to lay out the correct distance, and inserted another peg, "See? That's the width of the hall."

The two friars nodded.

Tossing the scale rule back into the pile, he told them, "I'm sailing to Malacca tomorrow. In the meantime, scale off the drawings like I had shown you, and lay out the plan of the church. Then get the masons to build. I'll be away maybe six months, so I expect to see progress when I return!"

"Are you sure?" the foreman asked, puzzled.

"That's what it says," Brother Guido replied.

The two men were standing on the site, setting out the church. As the width had already been pegged by Xavier, they were now laying out the length of the church, bay by bay.

"Are you sure the buttress is *that* thick?" the foreman asked, again. "It doesn't *look* that big on the drawing. It seems narrower."

"Your senses deceive you," Brother Guido replied sternly. "You must have faith."

The foreman shrugged. They continued, laying out one bay after the other. By the end of the day, they had laid out the entire church.

"It looks awfully long," the foreman said. "Much longer than in the drawing."

"It just *looks* long. An optical illusion caused by the fading light. Your senses are deceiving you!" Brother Guido told him, crossly. "Look, I had measured every dimension twice over, there's no mistake!"

"Okay, I have faith in you," the foreman said. "Just don't send me to the Inquisition, okay?"

Construction started. The lower levels were built of coral stone, the upper portion of brick, but as the walls rose, the foreman went off to search for Brother Guido.

"Where is Brother Guido?" he asked Brother Guillermo.

"He's sick today," Brother Guillermo told him. "I'm taking over. What do you want?"

"I need to know the height of the walls, windows and buttresses."

Brother Guillermo took out the architect's elevation, and laid a scale rule on it. He read off the heights of the various elements.

"Are you sure?" the foreman wondered. "Seems rather low to me."

Brother Guillermo bristled, "Are you questioning my measurement?"

The foreman decided to shut up. He had no intention of being part of the next *auto-da-fe,* where they burnt people alive for asking questions. Instead, he jotted the dimensions down on the back of his hand, and went off to instruct his workers.

As the walls neared completion, the foreman propped the drawings on a stand, and looked from them to the building, back and forth, comparing one against the other. *It didn't look right.* The buttresses were incredibly thick, the church was too long, and the facade too low and squat… but maybe it was true, his senses *were* deceiving him. Who was he to argue?

After nine months, Francis Xavier returned, and instantly had a fit.

"How could you build such a ridiculous church?" he screamed at the foreman. "Too long and so squat! It looks like a toad!"

The foreman shrugged and pointed to the two monks, "They gave me the dimensions."

Xavier glared at his two assistants.

"I read off the dimensions using the scale rule, just as you had shown us!" Brother Guido cried. He laid his scale rule on the plan. "See?"

Xavier stared at the scale rule. He read off the markings. All in order. It seemed to be correct, until he noticed letterings on the edge of the ruler: 1/8" to 1'-0".

He grabbed the architect's letter, which specified… 1/4" to 1'-0".

"Idiot!" he screamed. "You used the wrong scale rule!"

The two friars blanched.

"And what scale rule did *you* use for measuring the height?" Xavier demanded of Brother Guillermo.

"Umm…" Brother Guillermo stammered, and timidly held out the scale rule he used: 1/2" to 1'-0".

Xavier fainted.

In retrospect, it was obvious what had happened. To scale off the plan, Brother Guido had used a scale *half* the correct one, and the dimensions he read off were therefore *twice* what they should have been. Thus, he had stretched the church to twice its correct length, making it 360 feet long instead of 180 feet. This mistake also made each buttress twice as fat as it should have been.

Brother Guillermo had made the opposite mistake. He used a scale *twice* the correct one, and the heights he announced were only *half* of what were intended. In short (no pun intended) he made the church much too low. Along the way, the pointed Gothic arches were transmuted into round-top

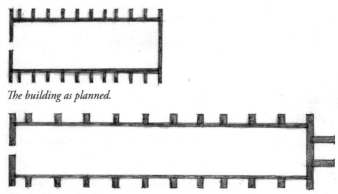

The building as planned.

The building as built.

classical ones. The Renaissance had finally arrived, albeit in a mutated form.

Even today, first-year architectural students make the same boo-boo. Whenever a tutor discovers this, the student must be beaten to death with his scale rule. But the two monks were not eighteen-year-old freshies but fully-grown men – and should have known better.

What was intended.   *What was actually built.*

Ironically, the foreman was correct all along. Unlike the two monks, the foreman had an innate sense of proportion. His eyes had *not* deceived him, and he should have trusted his senses – faith or no faith – and blew the whistle.

After defrocking and sending the two monks back to Spain in chains, Xavier gave up on his misshapen church. In any case, money had run out and he was *not* going to the Vatican to ask for more. Instead, he focused his attention on sending the young seminarians to China.

"The Chinese eat everything," he reasoned. "They would have no issue with Transubstantiation!" He was wrong: the Chinese ate everything, but they ate it *cooked*. As Xavier was not willing to hand over Jesus roasted, baked, steamed, stir-fried or flambéed, he had limited success.

We now fast-forward a century. In 1694, Father Antonio Estavillo of the Augustinian Order arrived in Paoay to set up a mission. "So *that's* the misshapen church," he remarked to his staff. "How the Jesuits really messed up!" (Note: Augustinians had no love for the Jesuits. *Their* order stretched all the way back to 1244, and regarded the Jesuits as recent and unruly upstarts.)

The little party gazed at the half-built hulk, now blackened and stained. "Actually Father, it's kind of cute," a young Augustinian remarked. "It reminds me of a squirrel that lived in a tree near my room, its cheeks bulging with nuts."

"Do we tear it down?" another asked.

Father Estavillo thought, and said, "Why waste it? It's already there. The City of God doesn't come cheap, and we got to begin somewhere… Besides, I like squirrels."

In fact, it was the easiest church they ever built: an instant church, just add a roof. Father Estavillo hired local carpenters who erected internal pillars, a roof, and set up an altar. They named the church after the founder of their order, Saint Augustine of Hippo.

At first, they made use of only the east-end of the church, but as the town expanded and more space was needed, they added more roof to the rest, extending the church westward, reaching the squashed (but rather cute) facade by 1710.

As Father Estavillo said, "Sometimes you *should* trust your senses, especially the common one."

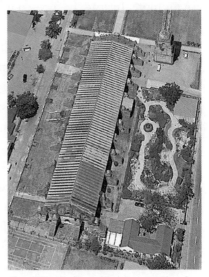

Google Earth photo of San Agustin Church.

20 VILLA IRREGOLARE

The Italian architect Andrea Palladio (1508 - 1580) is celebrated for his careful attention to proportion, dimensions, and above all, for his devotion to symmetry. Most famous of all his work is the Villa Rotonda, a country house outside Vicenza, which had inspired generations of English copycats and whose influence even extended to the nascent United States. The house is a perfect square, with all four facades exactly identical, and a dome in the precise middle.

What could be more perfectly symmetrical?

Alas, the truth was that in his later years, Palladio had become totally and utterly bored by symmetry. We know that because Giorgio Vasari (1511-1574), author of *Lives of the Most Excellent Painters, Sculptors and Architects,* continued to take notes even in his old age, intending a follow-up Volume Two that never got published. Among his gossipy and (by modern standards) libelous reports was one of Palladio screaming, "I loathe symmetry! Left is the same! Right is the same! I am so bored!"

Therefore, when priest Paolo Almerico retired in 1565 to his hometown of Vicenza and hired Palladio to design him a country house, Palladio saw it as a golden opportunity to launch into a radically new 'picturesque' direction.

Palladio designed a house that was determinedly asymmetric. It had a dome on the east, and only one of the four porticos was in line with the dome. The other three were aggressively off-centre and not of the same size. The rooms were also irregularly disposed. However, the response from the client was less than enthusiastic.

"What is this big room for?" Almerico asked.

"It is for Your Excellency's audiences."

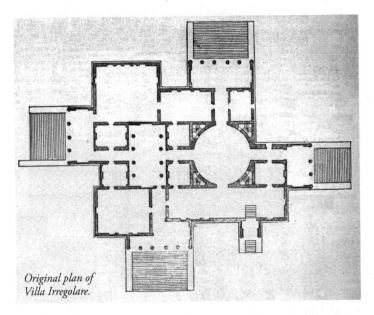

Original plan of Villa Irregolare.

"I… give audiences? The bishop will excommunicate me! Take it out," instructed the priest. "And, what is this room in the middle with eight dots?"

"Excellency, it is the Hall of Columns," Palladio replied. "Those dots are columns. Doric, Ionic, Corinthian and Tuscan. Two of each. All the classical orders in one room!"

"But, what is the room for?"

"It is to exhibit Your Excellency's collection of ancient Roman statues, of course."

Almerico blushed. "My collection is not one that would gladly see the light of day."

"That is why the room is in the middle," Palladio said soothingly. "No windows."

"Then how do I see them?" the elderly priest demanded.

The review of the design, already off on a rocky start, got worse. The priest then turned his attention to a long gallery that ran along the south side, which – oddly – had a small porch, situated at a level halfway between the upper and lower floors.

"This is your picture gallery," Palladio said. "To display the portraits of your ancestors."

"Very well, but why is there a small porch here?"

"Excellency, it is an entrance for your cats." (The priest was a well-known cat-lover.)

"But the steps extend *into* the gallery?!"

"Ah! If all the steps are outside, it would raise up the porch too high, and out of proportion, so I arranged to have it rise up to mid-level."

"And the rest of the steps intrude into the gallery? Do you mean to say that whilst I am walking around inside, I can fall into the stairwell?"

"We can put up a balustrade," Palladio answered desperately.

"Forget it. My cats never use the doors anyway. They jump through windows."

One by one, Palladio's eccentricities got knocked away. Almerico took out the Hall of Columns, Audience Room, feline porch and shortened the picture gallery – which reduced the plan to a square. The only irregularity left – which Palladio hung on to desperately – was the four porches of different sizes.

Palladio died in 1580, a disappointed man, but worse was to come. In 1592, the almost-completed villa was ceded to the Capri brothers, who appointed Palladio's assistant, Vincenzo Scamozzi, to finish it. When the two brothers visited the construction site, however, they made one final change.

South facade as originally designed. Note the cat-porch on the right side.

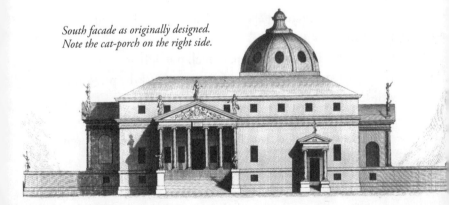

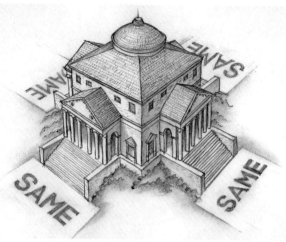

The Villa Rotonda as actually built, boringly symmetrical.

The older brother decided to live in the south side, whilst the younger took the north; their wives would take the east and west sides respectively. However, the portico on the east was distinctly smaller. Knowing their wives, the two brothers ordered all porticos to be made *exactly* the same. "Hell has no fury like a wife with a smaller porch," they wisely opined.

Thus, by an ironic twist of fate, the most irregular and 'picturesque' design Palladio ever produced was reduced to *the* most cold and boringly symmetrical one. An even greater irony was that it became an architectural icon – universally admired and much-imitated.

But the final insult to injury came when William Morris, the nineteenth century founder of the Arts and Crafts Movement, was shown Palladio's original drawings.

"The fool should have put in a few turrets," Morris sniffed.

21 MASECTOMY MAHAL

The Taj Mahal is both an icon of India and a symbol of romantic love, visited by millions of starry-eyed visitors every year. What most do not know – and probably would *rather* not know – is that the Taj Mahal exists in a sadly truncated form. The original design was very different from what we actually see today; for it was meant to have, not one, but *two* identical domes.

When Shah Jahan's favourite wife Mumtaz Mahal died during childbirth in 1631, the Mughal emperor was inconsolable (although, from her point of view it was a blessed release, since it was her fourteenth pregnancy). He resolved to build the grandest and most beautiful tomb in the world, to house her remains, and his own. The mausoleum was to have two identical domes, side by side, symbolising her two perfect breasts. She was to be buried under one dome, and of course the other dome was reserved for the Shah himself.

However, his architect Hassan Al Qibbal objected vehemently to the idea. Mughal architecture often featured multiple domes on one building, but a single, central dome always predominated. There was no precedence for a building with two domes of equal size.

"A building with two domes is as monstrous as a body with two heads," Al Qibbal opined.

Pregnant again.

The Shah replied mildly that if the architect did not do as he was told, he would find his own dome missing. The design was completed in a record five days. Within two months, construction started.

The two domes were supported by eight main arches; the two in the middle were parallel, thus visually uniting the spaces under the two domes. If the building had been completed that way, it could have created a truly new and innovative expression of space.

Unfortunately, it was not to be.

The dome on the left, intended for Mumtaz, was completed first, for her burial could not be deferred much longer. (Abdul Hamid Lahori commented that her 'fragrance' was starting to 'get a little strong'.) Her remains were placed in a vault deep underground, and a cenotaph was placed on the main floor, above her body, and directly under the centre of the dome.

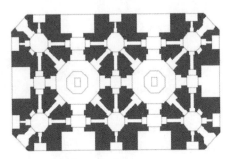

Original plan of the Taj Mahal.

By 1640, work started on the second dome. Unfortunately, when the building reached the level of the drum there was a catastrophic collapse. The dome caved in, burying fifty workers alive. It seemed that the Shah's impatience caused them to build too rapidly, imposing weight upon the arches whilst the mortar was still green. Needless to say, Al Qibbal was quickly relieved of *his* dome.

Simulation of what the Taj Mahal would have looked like, based on the original design.

The damage to the first dome was repaired, but the second dome was never rebuilt. For by now Shah Jahan had moved on to an even more ambitious scheme, one that involved a separate tomb for himself, facing the Taj Mahal from across the Yamuna River.

However, this meant all the minarets, garden, pools and the enclosing walls on the right of the Taj Mahal had to be demolished and rebuilt, so that the central axis would pass precisely through the remaining dome, instead of between the two domes as originally planned – *perfect symmetry must be preserved*, even though poor Mumtaz had received, so to speak, a mastectomy. The sadly truncated Taj Mahal was completed in 1648, and the last of the 4,934,567 cavities were filled with inlays of semi-precious stone, whereupon the craftsmen left the site and started new careers as dentists.

As for Shah Jahan's own tomb, a great deal of mystery surrounded its design, as the drawings and model had perished. A Persian historian railed against it: "Such filth, such utter obscenity as never before shamed the eyes of an empire!" Saadullah Khan was more delicate; he hinted in his journal that: "As the Queen's tomb embodied the female principle, the King's tomb will express the male principle." Abdul Hamid Lahori recorded that when the model was unveiled before the Emperor's counsellors: "There was total dead silence. Even his Hindu advisors, accustomed to the lingam, were left quite speechless."

Gathering all the vague descriptions and dark hints, we can surmise that Shah Jahan's tomb was shaped like a giant phallus – and probably quite graphic; there were some references to a 'fountain at the very tip'…

Despite the objections from his counsellors, Shah Jahan pressed on with his plans, but he never got beyond the foundations. In 1658, his son Aurangzeb overthrew and imprisoned him. He lived on in confinement, but his death in 1666 triggered a crisis, for there was no tomb prepared for him.

Aurangzeb proposed to place his father's remains in the Taj Mahal, but his architect pointed out that Mumtaz's sarcophagus already occupied the exact centre of the dome, so another one placed next to it would, of course, be off-centre, thus spoiling the perfect symmetry.

Aurangzeb retorted, "Well, put him *on top* of her. That's what he wanted, right?"

To this day, historians debate whether Aurangzeb was serious, or merely making a joke in very poor taste. The present author is inclined to the former, since there is no sign that Aurangzeb ever showed the slightest trace of humour. In any case, his horrified counsellors persuaded him to place his father's sarcophagus next to Mumtaz – decency being more important than symmetry.

What irony – if Shah Jahan knew that his own corpse would be the *one* thing that would ruin the perfection of his creation, no doubt he would have chosen burial at sea.

22 INVERTED FUNNEL

The dome of St Paul's Cathedral, soaring serenely over the City of London, is considered Christopher Wren's finest achievement – a model for countless other domes, from Washington to Singapore.

And yet, it is a *lie*. A beautiful, elegant lie – but a shameful, shameless sham, nonetheless.

St Paul's Cathedral.

Dome of St Paul's Cathedral –
a shameless lie.

The dome of the Cathedral has two layers: inner and outer. Filippo Brunelleschi also built the dome of the Florence Cathedral in two layers, but his double-domes were structural and functional: they actually covered the space and supported the lantern. A section across Wren's dome, however, reveals a cunning deceit. Hidden between the two layers is a brick *cone* that sits on top of the drum and supports the stone lantern above. The inner dome, with all its painted angels, is only a thin shell supported by the brick cone, and the outer dome is merely flimsy framework supporting curved lead sheets, prominent on the London skyline. In short, both domes are fakes.

My admiration for Wren took a nosedive when I discovered this. How *could* he? How could he stoop to such fakery, such deceit, such hanky-panky?

The original St Paul's Cathedral was medieval, with a tower over the crossing. During the reign of James I, architect Inigo Jones attempted to re-clad it in the more fashionable Classical style, but never got beyond some porches with volutes. The church remained in this half-Gothic, half-Classical state through the next two reigns – Charles I, who lost his head, and Oliver Cromwell, who lost his temper (which accounted for Charles I losing his head). It remained thus when Charles II was restored to the throne, but *everything* – Gothic and Classical – burnt down in the Great Fire of London, 1666.

Charles II ordered Wren to design a new church. Wren's first design was a dome over a Greek cross, with four equal arms. Architects like Greek crosses; aside from it being perfectly symmetrical, it saved them the trouble of designing a nave.

The burning cathedral, 1666. Note Inigo Jones' classical porches on the transept.

However, the members of the church didn't see it that way. "A *Greek* cross, Master Wren?" the Archbishop of Canterbury snorted. "What do you think we are, pray? We're Anglicans, for Heaven's sake, not Greek Orthodox!"

Back to the drawing board. Wren lengthened one arm by adding a small dome, thus creating a sort of nave. To sell the design, he ordered a wooden model. Today, it is still on display. But once again, the design was rejected.

"Forsooth, what is this big round thing?" the Bishop of Ely muttered. "Queer sort of roof."

"Your Grace, it is a *dome*," Wren replied.

"We English don't do domes," the Archbishop of Canterbury replied, testily. "We build steeples. Now, take the one at Salisbury – a nice, good old-fashioned *English* steeple. Can you not give us one of those?"

The Great Model.

"Indeed," the Bishop of Bath added. "This thing looks like an egg with stripes. And pray, why is it wearing a pepper pot to boot?"

"Your Grace, it is modelled after Michelangelo's dome in Rome," Wren explained.

If this was intended as justification, it backfired. The hall was thrown into turmoil. Shocked cries of "Roman!" and "Papist!" arose from all sides. "A Catholic plot!" someone hissed. "Throw him in gaol!"

Narrowly escaping with his life, Wren next produced a conventional Latin cross on plan but with a strange feature at the crossing. Wren reversed his dome, putting the dome below and the drum on top of it, with a strange, stepped steeple above it.

The churchmen looked at it in silence.

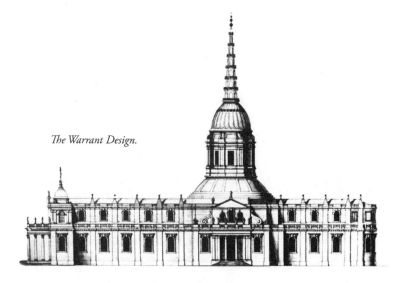

The Warrant Design.

"Is this a steeple, pray?" the Archbishop of Canterbury pointed to the top.

"Your Grace did ask for a steeple," Wren muttered.

"Forsooth, it looks more like a Chinese pagoda," the Bishop of Bath remarked.

"We Anglicans don't do pagodas," some other bishop murmured.

Wren said desperately, "It is an English steeple expressed in Classical form."

The King pulled Wren aside and hissed, "Methinks we've seen this drawing before. It is your plan to re-clad the *old* St Paul's, is it not? Do you think we cannot recognise Inigo Jones' porches with those curly volutes?"

Wren, ashen, nodded, "I know Your Majesty is most anxious to start work, so I dusted off some old drawings…" He glanced around to see if anyone was listening, and continued, "When work starts, I promise to revise it!"

The King nodded. Returning to the churchmen – who were still firing pot-shots at the drawing – he cut short the argument, "Silence! We warrant this design." He stamped the Great Seal upon the paper and signed it with a flourish. "Now get the work started!"

During the construction, from 1675 to 1720, Wren – with the King's backing – made changes to the design, gradually evolving into the actual building we see today.

This, at least, was the conventional version of its history…

In 2007, whilst working on a secret project to install missile silos in the Tower of London, I was told the truth at last. (If it occurred to you that the Tower of London does not have missiles, it only shows that you don't know everything, and I'm not telling you anything more…)

A member of MI5 (who asked to remain nameless, so I shall call him 'Nameless' hereon) learnt of my interest in the Cathedral. After swearing me to secrecy, he brought a folder. "Have you heard of a chap called Samuel Pepys?" he asked.

"Samuel Pepys?" I answered. "Didn't he keep a diary? A nasty, sordid, scandalous diary –

Samuel Pepys where angels fear to tread,
Upon little Nell earning her daily bread."

Nameless snorted, "Fine, you know some history, or at least the gossips. Now read this." He opened the folder and extracted a printout. "Pepys wrote part of his diary in code. Mostly about his sex life he didn't want his wife to know about. However, there were two passages in a very difficult code, and it was not deciphered for centuries – until we set two of our Cray supercomputers upon it."

"*Two* Crays!" I exclaimed. "It must've been one tough code!"

"The first computer *exploded*. Now read it and you'll know why."

"His Majesty swore us to secrecy, for the King of France must not learn of this, and make us the laughing-stock of Europe; and yet it is so quaint I cannot resist, so I am writing it in code, with only myself knowing the keyword, so that in my old age I can spend my last days cackling by the fireplace…

Today we assembled at the worksite of the Cathedral. When His Majesty arrived, he gazed upon the drum, which is a circle of elegant Corinthian columns, but rising above it, is a curious cone of brick, supporting the lantern on its tip. Espying a workman applying gold leaf upon the cone, he exclaimed, 'Forsooth, Mr Wren! Why do you add gilding, which shall be concealed afterwards by the dome? Is that not a waste?'

Mr Wren bowed and said, 'Your Majesty, there will be no dome.'

'Surely you are not exposing this cone?' the Archbishop exclaimed.

'Your Grace, the Anglican Faith embodies the truth of God, so must the church be truthful! The cone is all we need. It fulfils its function of covering the space below and lifting the lantern high! I do propose some gilding, for God will surely forgive us a little Embellishment, so long as we proclaim the Truth of Materials... His Majesty had approved this design already.'

'We have not!' the King exclaimed. 'We never approved this monstrosity!'

'But Your Majesty has!' cried Mr Wren. From his satchel he pulled out a drawing. It was an elevation of the church, but rising above the drum, is curiously perverted object, an inverted cone. Mr Wren turned the drawing over and lo! – on the back was the stamp of the Great Seal, and the King's signature, albeit a trifle wobbly.

'I did not approve this!' the King cried, forgetting the royal 'we'. 'I only signed the Warrant Design!'

'Well, we shall call this the Unwarranted Design,' the Dean whispered.

'T'is a fraud!' the King exclaimed. 'I certainly do not recall this!'

'But I do!' said Mistress Nell Gwyn, who had been observing from the edge. She curtsied and said, 'Does Your Majesty not remember, it was on the very night I was proclaimed the 'Protestant Whore'?'

'What is this, pray?' muttered the Bishop of Exeter, perplexed.

'Your Grace may pray, but being a man of the cloth, you may not have heard. Well, that night I was in my coach, when I heard people shouting, 'Whore! Get back to France, ye Catholic whore!' They had mistaken me for that French slut, Louise de Kerouaille. So, I leaned out of the coach and cried, 'Be silent, good people, I am the Protestant Whore!'

The Unwarranted Design.

'I was not aware, Madam, that you had become a soldier of our church,' the Archbishop said, sarcastically.

'Alas!' Nell smiled. 'I admit I cannot shoot arrows or muskets. I am but the target, for His Majesty's good practice.'

'Nell!' the King cried. 'I prithee, what has this to do with the matter?'

'Had Your Majesty forgotten? We were celebrating my new title with our fifth toast, when Mr Wren came in with this drawing. And Your Majesty stamped it most heartily!'

'Nell, you must have been drunk!' the King muttered.

'Drunk!' she cried. 'Your Majesty wielded the Great Seal with such gusto you nearly crushed his fingers! Do you not recall that night?'

'Nell, I swear to you, I have absolutely no memory…'

'And the next morning you thought I was Moll Davis.'

'Oh,' the King turned pink. 'That *night*.'

'Yes, that night. I see Your Majesty does not know one whore from the next, Protestant or otherwise,' Nell remarked scathingly.

At this point, the Archbishop tried to steer the topic back to more elevated matters. 'Mr Wren, are you proposing a conical roof upon the church?'

'Aye, your Grace, for the Form must fulfil the Function it serves! In any case, had Your Grace not objected to a dome as being too Papist, and desired a steeple instead?'

'Mr Wren!' the Bishop of Ely cut in. 'This thing is hardly a steeple.'

'More like an inverted funnel,' the Bishop of Coventry noted.

We all gazed, and I suppressed a giggle, for the cone, with its cylindrical lantern, did look rather like an inverted funnel.

'Enough!' the King roared. 'Mr Wren, you shall build me a proper dome. Who has ever heard of a building wearing a blasted funnel upon its head?'

'Why, I never wear my funnel on my head,' Nell added sweetly.

'Your funnel, Nell?' the King asked, suspiciously. 'I never see you with any funnel.'

'I wear mine a little lower down. Your Majesty knows where – you've visited it often enough!' With a bound and a skip she jumped into the coach, shouting, 'To Haymarket, ho! This funnel needs another barrel!'

I heard a crash behind – the Bishop of Coventry had fainted. Whilst we undid his collar, the King bore down upon Mr Wren with a face of thunder, 'Mr Wren, you shall put a proper dome upon the church.'

'Your Majesty! We must observe the Truth of Materials! What will they say when we add a piece of fakery…'

'Mr Wren, you shall add a dome!'

Wren, white-faced, whispered, 'I shan't!'

The King looked like a volcano about to explode. 'I have in mind to build myself a pleasure palace on Crumbledore-upon-Scree. As you are the Surveyor for the Crown, you will get thee hither and start your scribblings. Now!'

As the King stalked away, Mr Wren collapsed, and the meeting broke up in confusion.

Away to home, where I took out the Great Atlas of Greater Great Britain, and after an hour of perusal I found Crumbledore-upon-Scree. It is a scrap of an island, barely ten miles across, two hundred leagues north of the Shetlands. Its only produce is *brambles, and the inhabitants subsist on haggis, which (I hear) is made of leftover bagpipes filled with offal that the three witches of Macbeth had rejected. I shuddered for poor Mr Wren…"*

"No wonder the computer exploded!" I exclaimed. "If anyone could burn up a Cray supercomputer, it'll be Nell Gwyn. And poor old Wren! Trying to defend his design and got banished to the boonies! What happened next?"

Nameless pulled out another sheet from his folder. "There's more. I told you, there are *two* passages. This is the other entry, dated about a fortnight after the first…"

"The Lord be praised, all is well. Three days ago, Mr Wren returned and, upon his knees, humbly kissed His Majesty's hand. The King graciously forgave him, and even knighted the fellow, and returned him to the Works. This morning, as I passed the Cathedral, I was gratified to see frames being set up on the cone, forming a curved shape which shall be sheathed in lead. A dome at last!

But standing below, gazing up with a woebegone look, was Mr Wren himself – now Sir Christopher. I hailed him, but observing that he was very thin, I said, 'Why, Sir Christopher, you look unwell – quite thin and haggard!'

He turned upon me sad eyes, 'Now you know why they call it haggis. One more bite and I'll be naught but a haggard old hag…'

Then he cried, 'Oh, Master Pepys, why was I ever born? Why did I ever become an architect? I have sold my integrity! I settled for this false dome, this outrageous fakery, this vile deception!

I sold my truth – and for what? A knighthood and a pat on the head!'

A tear fell from his eyes, 'I am a whore, no less than Nell.'

I tried to console him, 'At least you tried your best. She may be a Protestant Whore, but you are at least a Protesting *whore.'*

I must say, this revelation restored my esteem of Wren. Although (they say) all architects are whores, at least *this* one tried to defend his values. If we can forgive Galileo for recanting, surely, we can look upon Wren's 'sell-out' with gentle eyes. After all, Galileo was merely threatened with the rack, but Wren nearly met a fate worse than death.

Amnesty International had declared English food 'a crime against humanity'; but even worse – *much* worse – was *Scottish* cooking.

23 NEITHER HERE NOR THERE

The abbey of Mont Saint-Michel was built upon one of nature's oddities: a craggy mountain off the shore of Normandy, surrounded by mudflats so gentle that twice a day the tide rushes in, and the mountain becomes an islet. When the tide retreats, it joins the mainland once more. Before the causeway was built in the nineteenth century, the mountain bounced daily from land to water, water to land – but in the seventeenth century, it managed to bounce all the way from Europe to Asia, and back again.

Land or water? East or West? French or Siamese?

In 1685, King Louis XIV of France sent a royal delegation headed by Duc de Chaumont to King Narai (the Great) of Siam, at his capital Ayutthaya. This was not the first time the Siamese saw white people. The Portuguese had arrived first, but they were dour, dressed in black and only wanted to talk religion, which bored the Siamese. The English also came, but they were dour, dressed in black and only wanted to talk business, which bore the Siamese even more.

Then, the French came. Whatever else one could have said about the French they did know how to put on a show. The French party was dressed in the height of fashion – embroidered waistcoats, periwigs, high heels, ribbons, jewels and mountains of lace. How they survived the tropical heat without melting remains a mystery. In any case they made a deep impression, and Narai agreed to let the French set up a base on the banks of the Chao Phraya River, near the capital.

However, Narai demanded reciprocity. If the French were to have a base in Siam, it was only fair that the Siamese have a similar base in France. After intense negotiation lasting three days, de Chaumont – anxious for a deal – agreed.

When Louis XIV received de Chaumont's report, he was appalled. It was one thing to have a convenient beachhead in a foreign country, from which a colonising invasion might be launched, it was an entirely different thing to let that foreign power have a similar beachhead in France. However, the treaty had already been signed, and although the King may scream, he would have to abide by it or face expulsion from Siam.

So, where to put the Siamese?

By a stroke of luck, the Abbot of Mont Saint-Michel had died the year before, and the monks were unable to elect a successor, being deeply divided between three candidates. Using the excuse of 'putting an end to all this wrangling', the King disbanded the monks, packed them off to various other monasteries, and reserved the abbey for the Siamese. It was a good solution: sufficiently far from Versailles to avoid Siamese meddling in politics, and sufficiently isolated to thwart any attempts at invasion. "If they want to invade France by land, they can only do it during *low* tide," Louis XIV gloated. "And if they want to invade by sea, they can only do it during *high* tide."

Thus, when the Siamese delegation arrived in France, they were courteously received at Versailles but were quickly whisked off to the bleak coasts of Normandy. There they found a deserted abbey on a desolate rock. The delegation headed by Phrayangchao Rattanadharma Na Ayutthaya (known to his friends as 'Bop') was disappointed and had little choice but to make the best of a bad deal.

Their first tour of the abbey was an example of culture shock. Knowing virtually nothing of Catholicism, they thought the statue of the Virgin was the Chinese Guanyin, but were confounded by a copy of Van Eyck's *Adoration of the Lamb*.

Adoration of the Lamb, detail.

"They worship animals?" Bop asked, looking at people prostrating to the lamb.

"It looks like a sheep," his Aide-de-Camp (known as 'Lek') replied, peering closely.

"I thought they *eat* sheep?"

"Maybe they eat what they worship. I heard they drink blood too, every Sunday."

"The French are crazy."

The first winter was terrible. The Siamese hated the cold and shivered even under layers of clothing. The food was worse. Having a limited budget, Bop could only afford to feed his staff vegetables, which they made into a kind of stew – cabbages, carrots, liberally showered with green peas. This diet became so monotonous that the soldiers sarcastically named it *'ratana-tua'* (jewel peas).

At spring, Lek had an idea. "Our King commanded us to make this place a showcase for Siam," he told Bop. "What if we converted this ugly stone church into a beautiful Siamese temple? Then everyone who sees it will want to visit Siam!"

It was the world's first experiment in tourism promotion. The Siamese – by now lonely, homesick and bored out of their minds – leapt at the idea. It was something to do, anyway. Taking apart a portion of their ship and buying more wood from the locals, they erected a second, steeper roof on top of the nave, the gable front decorated with *nagas* and curlicues, topped by a *cho-fah* (sky tassel), all lovingly carved and painted. The square stone tower over the crossing disappeared under multiple layers of overlapping roofs, snuggling up on all four sides. As for the steeple…

"We need a *phrang*," Bop remarked to Lek.

Using the steeple as an internal support, they added layers of wood cladding, terminating in a little spire. As spring progressed into summer, the ancient Gothic church disappeared under new Siamese dress, and re-emerged as *Wat Arun Pek* (Temple of the Morning Sheep). Even the flying buttresses – which they could not remove – received little *mandops* on the tips.

To be sure, it was not perfect. The *cho-fa* was a flat cut-out rather than three-dimensionally carved, and the *phrang* lacked the usual corner rebates. But given their lack of experience and shortage of material, it was a very creditable effort. Indeed, the building became a local curiosity, and a French artist published an engraving *(below)* of it. Even more unexpectedly, the vegetable stew *ratana-tua* became popular among the local peasantry, who found it tasty and affordable.

Mont Saint-Michel as it appeared in 1687 – a Gothic church in Siamese dress.

But sadly, it ended in failure. While the Siamese delegation was busily hammering away, relations back in Ayutthaya were turning sour. The French started to fortify their base, arousing the fears of the Siamese, and after Narai died, the French were told to leave.

As tit-for-tat, the French expelled the Siamese from the abbey, which was restored to the original monastic order. As Bop and his team sadly sailed away, they saw all the colourful Siamese trimmings torn down, and the abbey church reverted to its original grey and gloomy appearance. All their effort to promote Siam had gone to waste.

But the Siamese had the last laugh. Today, Siam – or Thailand (as it is now named) is one of the most-visited destinations in the world. Furthermore, their vegetable stew *ratana-tua* – after having undergone some local changes – eventually became popular throughout France, under a new name: *Ratatouille.*

Mont Saint-Michel today.

24 **EMPEROR IN A HOLE**

Millions of visitors enter Les Invalides to visit Napoleon Bonaparte's tomb, only to stop short in puzzlement: "Where's the tomb?" Only when they look down do they discover that the tomb is indeed there, but unlike all other tombs, it is *set into a hole,* in the centre of the church.

So how did the great Emperor sink so low?

Les Invalides was commissioned by Louis XIV as a hospital and retirement home for his veteran soldiers. A site was chosen on the plains of Grenelle, then a suburban part of Paris. The architect, Liberal Bruant, completed the construction by 1676, despite the King's suspicion of his name. "Never trust a liberal," he muttered.

The complex consisted of two wings containing living quarters, and in the space between, was a chapel for the veterans.

Later, the King decreed a royal chapel for himself; and of course, it had to be grander than the chapel for mere veterans. Jules Hardouin-Mansart, who had taken over from the elderly

Bruant, added a square building, topped by a dome, and placed back-to-back with the veteran chapel, separated by a screen. "Saves operating cost," the King said. "Only one priest needed." This enormous royal chapel – known as 'Eglise du Dome' – was completed in 1708, and its gilded dome became a landmark of the city.

And after a while, it began to smell.

What Mansart did not know – and Liberal Bruant did not tell him – was that during the construction of the first phase, temporary latrines for the workmen were built in the space

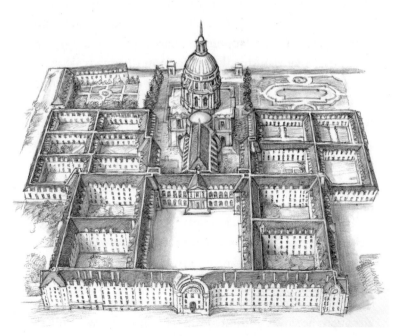

Les Invalides, with the domed royal chapel in the middle.

between the two wings, just beyond the end of the veteran's chapel. Below the latrines was an underground cesspool. When the works were completed the latrines were removed but the cesspool remained. All the same it did not smell, being sealed and underground, and as time went on it was simply... forgotten.

Never trust a liberal.

By sheer bad luck, Mansart's church was built directly above the cesspool, with the dome overhead. The cesspool was not discovered because the foundations of the piers were sunk *around* it but did not intrude into it. The floor above was paved over with marble, and the cesspool was thus entombed under the church. Out of sight, out of mind, but unfortunately, not out of smell.

As the years went by, the gasses from the slowly decaying mass started to seep up, escaping between the paving stones. At first the smell was barely detectable, and most people blamed it on the veterans, whose personal habits were somewhat lamentable. But by the reign of Louis XVI, it had become quite noticeable; Marie Antoinette flatly refused to attend any services there. "I get more smells than I want at *Versailles*," she declared. "I don't need any more!"

In 1789, revolutionaries attacked Les Invalides – but sickened by the smell, they transferred their attention to the Bastille instead. (Too bad; otherwise the French would be celebrating Invalid Day instead of Bastille Day.)

By the early 1800s, the smell had gotten quite strong, although the slow diffusion meant that the source was difficult to pin down. Napoleon attended a service, and apparently didn't mind the smell. Immediately afterwards he wrote to Josephine: "Am coming home soon. Don't wash."

Napoleon became Emperor, inheriting the mantle of Absolutism from the Bourbons, but found that his power was not as absolute as he desired. In 1815, he lost the Battle of Waterloo and was exiled to the island of St Helena, where he died in 1821.

In 1830, the July Revolution did away with Charles X and the new King, Louis Philippe, promptly closed down the church, as by then the stench had become quite unbearable.

Why did the smell persist so long? Most probably the cesspool was almost airtight, and the decomposition took place slowly but over a very long time. It was rotting in slow motion. However, the lack of airflow also meant that gasses accumulated, and pressure slowly built up.

In 1835, Louis Philippe ordered the reluctant architect Louis Visconti to do an investigation. After eliminating every other cause, Visconti got his workers to dig downwards. In his diary he recounted:

"... after we removed the paving and dug down a few feet, we heard a rumbling sound and suddenly the entire floor heaved upwards, and a fountain of unspeakable brownish material shot up in the air, along with the stench of a thousand pigsties. I thought a volcano had erupted, right inside the church. We stumbled outside and threw up. Some of the workmen thought that Hell had ruptured forth, but I fervently hope that, if I should ever end up there, it would be merely fire and brimstone and not that horrendous stench..."

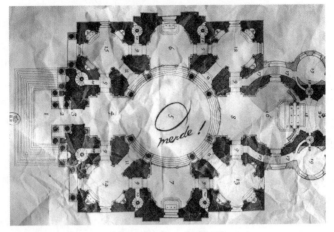

Approximate location of the cesspool, marked by Visconti.

The location of the newly-discovered cesspool was marked on a report to Louis Philippe, in somewhat inelegant language, but Visconti was understandably upset.

It took six months and fifty tons of lime to clean up the mess, during which Visconti had to double the pay of his workers, not only because of the appalling smell but to ensure their silence. A hoarding was built around the church, and the roads passing in front were closed 'for repairs' to keep the public beyond smelling distance. The entire cesspool, complete with its stone lining, had to be laboriously removed and carefully carted out at night, leaving a huge hole in the middle of the church.

In the meantime, Louis Philippe asked Prince de Joinville to bring Napoleon's remains back to France, no doubt hoping to associate himself with the great Emperor. This was done with great pomp and ceremony. But Louis Philippe found himself treading a thin line, as there were many in France with republican sentiments who did *not* welcome the return of a tyrannical Emperor.

So, where to bury Napoleon? The Pantheon was the obvious place, but there was no question of him occupying a small, ordinary crypt, like Voltaire – and it was doubtful the two corpses would appreciate each other's company: one was an absolute monarch and the other absolutely couldn't keep his mouth shut. Louis Philippe planned a grand tomb in the middle of the Pantheon but was met with noisy objections from liberals and republicans. (Never, *ever* trust a liberal). Louis Philippe was in a dilemma, having painted himself into the proverbial corner.

It was a chance meeting between Prince de Joinville and Visconti that solved the problem. The Prince was passing Les Invalides when he saw the architect emerge, with a hangdog expression. He stopped his carriage to ask the reason, and Visconti explained, after swearing the Prince to secrecy. Then they discussed the problem of Napoleon's tomb, which was troubling the Prince. Visconti recalled:

"… and suddenly, we both stopped and stared at each other. An utterly insane thought passed between us, even though neither of us said a word. Then, as one, we both turned and looked towards Les Invalides, and the Prince muttered, 'A perfect solution!'

'I thought the idea was to put him in the Pantheon?' I asked.

'That would imply he was a great man, so those damned

liberals are screaming. But Les Invalides houses old veterans, so putting him here would honour him as a great soldier. Even the liberals cannot dispute that!'

'But all the same, they would object that a big grand tomb would over-glorify him...'

'Why do you think God gave us a hole in the ground?'"

Louis Philippe was at his wit's end and consented. The big hole left by the cesspool was reshaped into a circle, surrounded by square columns with marble angels, and Napoleon was ceremoniously placed inside a giant sarcophagus in the exact middle.

It *was* the perfect solution. The tomb was big enough to satisfy the Bonapartists, sufficiently out of sight to satisfy the liberals; and if there was any residual smell, contemplate Lord John Acton's words: "Power corrupts, and absolute power is a real stinker."

Napoleon's tomb, sunk inside a former cesspool.

25 A COLOURFUL HISTORY

In the middle of Malacca, Malaysia stands a church. Officially known as Christ Church, it is invariably dubbed the 'Red Church' by locals. A Communist plot? A Marxist conspiracy? Not at all. The church and the surrounding buildings are, indeed, red – a deep, russet red.

If you ask the locals, they will blush and tell you the church was painted red simply because they liked it so. *They are lying.* In fact, the church had an embarrassing but colourful history, and had undergone more colour changes than a chameleon. At various times it was known as the 'Bloody Church', 'Orange Church', 'Triple-coloured Church', 'Yellow Church' and so on…

In 1511, the Portuguese colonised Malacca, and on top of a hill Francis Xavier built the Church of Saint Paul. Apparently, he was so busy travelling that he forgot to roof it, and roofless it remains to this day. So, when the Dutch seized Malacca, the Dutch burghers naturally objected to worshipping there, and proceeded to build a new Protestant church in the city.

The Red Church.

The effort was spearheaded by the Deputy Governor of Malacca, Claas de Wind, and the foundation stone was laid by his son Abraham. But when it was nearing completion, the local community was thrown into crisis by events back in the Netherlands.

In 1751, William IV, Prince of Orange, died. His young son became the new Stadtholder, and a regency council was formed to rule in his name. But there were dark rumours of a power struggle, even a possible coup d'état to overthrow the House of Orange, to replace it with a republic.

de Wind gathered the community in the Town Hall and harangued the burghers, "We must prove our loyalty to the House of Orange!" The speech lasted five hours and the weary burghers, anxious to go home, agreed to paint the emblem of the House of Orange on the front wall of the church.

The church was just receiving its final coat of whitewash, so de Wind summoned the paint contractor Premadassa Singh, a migrant from Tamil Nadu whose command of the Dutch language was somewhat shaky.

"Paint the Orange emblem on the wall," de Wind instructed.

Puzzled, Prem went to his son, "What is 'emblem'?"

His son checked the dictionary. "It means 'a picture or symbol'…"

Prem scratched his head. "I know an orange, but why should anyone want a *picture* of an orange?"

"Dad, the customer is always right," his son replied. "No matter how crazy."

Prem proceeded to mix a big batch of orange paint. No emulsion paint in those days could achieve that color, so Prem used a base of linseed oil, adding to it a mixture of pigments. This created a bright orange paint which hardened quickly. Erecting his scaffold on the porch, he painted…

"An orange?!!" the elder de Wind screamed, appalled. "He painted a *fruit* on the church?"

"Well, you did tell him 'Orange'," Abraham drawled.

Prem was thrown in jail whilst father and son argued over what to do.

"It doesn't even look like an orange," de Wind sniffed. "More like a tangerine."

"What's the difference?" Abraham asked.

"Tangerines are soft-skinned. You can peel it with your fingernails. Try doing that to an orange," de Wind said. "Oranges have thick skins. And, they are usually sour."

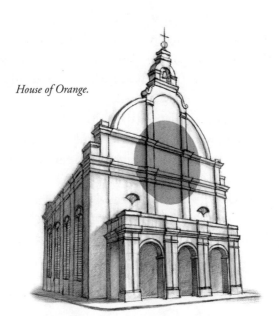

House of Orange.

Abraham secretly wrote to William V that his father called the House of Orange 'thick-skinned and sour'. Enraged, the young Stadtholder charged de Wind with *lèse-majesté* and ordered him back to Amsterdam, in chains. "I'll flay him and we'll see who has thick skin!" he screamed, not realising that he had already proven himself thin-skinned.

Abraham was made the Acting Deputy Governor – exactly what he intended. However, he did not gloat for long, since he was confronted with a new crisis: *the church started to bleed.*

Red patches started to appear, like bruises. Worse, streaks of red started to extend down from the cornices, like bloodstains. Was this Heaven protesting against Abraham's perfidy?

Reality was simpler. Whitewash was a mixture of lime powder and water, and the water came from a newly-dug well nearby. Unknown to the users, however, the water was heavily charged with dissolved iron, in the ferrous state. It was invisible, but when exposed to air, it oxidised and turned into *ferric* oxide – which was red. In short, the church was rusting; and since the neighbouring buildings had all been whitewashed at the same time, they too were getting streaky.

The thriving centre of Malacca was turning into a rust-belt.

It would not have been so bad if the rusting had been even. But the micro-climate on different parts of the buildings varied – some received more sunlight, others more rain. The cornices dripped water on the walls below, but unevenly, resulting in a blood-streaked appearance.

Bloody but unbowed.

The burghers were furious. At a stormy council meeting, they blamed Abraham, who blamed Prem. "First, he gave us iron-stained whitewash! Then he painted a stupid orange! We should *kill* him!"

"Come to think of it," one of the calmer burghers mused. "How come his orange isn't blood-stained?"

It was true. Red streaks and splotches had appeared everywhere *except* on his bright orange fruit. The orange paint, being oil-based and impervious to water, did not allow the rust to seep through; it remained bright and unblemished. Ironically, Prem's second blunder solved the first.

Prem was released and told to paint *everything* orange. "The customer is always right," he muttered to his son, as they prepared a huge vat of orange paint.

Thus the 'Blood-stained Church' became the 'Orange Church'. The effect was startling, but cheerful; at least the locals could not complain of vitamin C shortage.

But seventy years later, they were confronted by another crisis.

The Dutch had colonies in Malacca (Malaya) and also Batavia (Java). But to their fury, the British grabbed Bencoolen in south Sumatra, next to Java. Adding insult to injury, Sir Stamford Raffles established Singapore at the tip of the Malay Peninsula, as if thumbing his nose at the Dutch.

It was the era of Imperialism, which meant everybody grabbed. The result of this frenzied grabbing was skewed geopolitics, especially the 'geo' part where nations ended up with crazy bits of this and that, far-flung, scattered and intermixed. This got cumbersome, so the Great Powers decided to do some serious horse-trading:

"If I give you Bencoolen," the Brits said to the Dutch. "What can you give me in return?"

"I'll trade you Malacca," the Dutch replied. "Their satays are really good."

"Can you throw in Batavia too?" the Brits asked, hopefully. "We like beef rendang."

"No way. But we'll promise not to blow up Singapore."

Officially, it was known as the Anglo-Dutch Treaty of 1824, but actually it was schoolboys swapping marbles. Of course, the locals had no say in the matter, so the news that Malacca had been sold to the British arrived like a thunderbolt to the stolid Dutch burghers of Malacca. Therefore, on his way back to England, Raffles stopped in Malacca, to calm ruffled feathers.

"Don't worry," Raffles told the grumpy burghers. "We won't feed you fish n' chips."

"You'll just force us to eat stone," the burghers whined.

"Do you mean 'scones'?" Raffles asked, puzzled.

"Same-same."

Raffles mused, "I daresay you are right. But look on the bright side. Better us than the Americans."

"Why? What's wrong with the Yankees?"

"If the Yanks took over, you burghers will have to eat burgers," Raffles chuckled.

"Don't *pun*-ish us," the Burghers grumbled.

However, Raffles was startled by the bright orange church.

"It's to honour the House of Orange," the burghers told him.

"How patriotic! But now that Malacca is British, orange won't do."

"Why not? Didn't you English once have a king from the House of Orange?"

"You mean William III, of 'William-and-Mary'," Raffles replied. "But he was king only because he *married* an English queen. Lucky fellow. But that house had died out. It's the House of Hanover now, you know."

"So, you English got handed over to the Hanover."

"Very funny," Raffles snorted. "Right! Are you now their *pun*-dits…"

Glaring at the Orange Church, Raffles demanded, "Who is the main paint contractor in this town?"

This was Sanjay Singh, great-grandson of Prem who inherited and expanded the family business. Sanjay grew up in Malacca and spoke Dutch fluently – and not a word of English.

Raffles was undeterred. As translators he used his Malay staff, Hassan, and Sitar, a Tamil housewife who also spoke Malay. Thus:

Raffles (in English): "We British don't want an orange church."

Hassan (in Malay): "British no like orange church."

Sitar (in Tamil): "They no like orange."

Sanjay (confused): "They want papaya?"

Raffles: "The British flag is the Union Jack."

Hassan: "British like Union Jack."
Sitar: "They want union with Jack."
Sanjay: "Who's Jack?"

Raffles: "The Union Jack is red, white, and blue."
Hassan: "Jack likes red, white, blue."
Sitar: "Red, white, blue."
Sanjay: "Red, white, blue. *Got it!*"

Sanjay summoned his team and got to work. Since the porch had three arches, and the wall above was divided by pilasters into three vertical panels, it was logical that Sanjay followed this natural division: the left side he painted red, the middle portion white, and the right side royal blue.

Sanjay was thrown into prison – as a suspected French agent.

Tricolor Church.

What Sanjay had inadvertently produced was the French Tricolor. This was a flag invented during the French Revolution by a seamstress named Marianne, who stitched together three colors: red, for courage; white, for purity; and blue, because she ran out of green cloth. In the picture below, painted by her lover Eugène Delacroix, she is seen leading the assault on Versailles, followed by her alarming little ten-year old brother Gaston, pistols in both fists and firing wildly in all directions.

Marianne invented the Tricolor.

After a week in jail, Sanjay was released. Raffles discovered that, aside from knowing no English, Sanjay knew not a word of French either. "Can't be a French agent," Raffles reasoned. "The French would never hire anyone who can't speak their blasted language."

Giving up on translators, he shoved a picture of the Union Jack into Sanjay's hands, and indicated, by sign language, what he wanted.

Union Jacked.

As history's first attempt on super-graphics, the result could only be considered a fair success; the church now looked like a giant blue box wrapped with red and white ribbons. The Dutch community grumbled but the British garrison was pleased. There was no longer any need to raise the flag every morning – it was already there.

But, the British ran into trouble. In 1831, Dol Said, chief of Naning district, rebelled against British taxes. The disturbances spread into Malacca, and the mixed community took this opportunity to protest British rule by spitting on the Union Jack, which meant spitting on the church. The riots were put down, but left a bad taste, so when Daniel Wilson, Bishop of Calcutta came in 1838 to re-consecrate the church, he was distinctly worried. "I've heard of jack-in-a-box," he mused. "But never Jack *on* a box!"

He repainted it bright yellow, in honour of his canary. Three months later came a thunderbolt from China. Daoguang Emperor sent an envoy to lodge an angry protest: yellow is the prerogative of the Chinese Imperial family. The furious Emperor threatened to expel all British nationals from Canton or worse, feed them dog meat.

Hurriedly, the Governor repainted it pale green. But that was not the end of the matter, for the local Malay community came to complain. "Green is *our* color," the Imam told the British. "Mohammed's cloak was green."

"Nobody has copyright on chlorophyll!" the Governor retorted.

"True, but it is causing confusion," the Imam grumbled. "Some of our members wandered in, thinking it a mosque, and found it pointing directly *away* from Mecca!"

"We had white, orange, red, white, blue, yellow and green," the Governor wailed. "What's left?"

"Why not violet?" the Imam suggested.

So, the church was painted a violent shade of violet. It looked like Barbara Cartland had puked on it, but there were no other colours left. It remained the 'Violet Church' without any further disturbances for the next several decades.

But by 1910, troubles started again. The walls developed wrinkles and creases, as if the masonry was crumbling, but inspection on the inside showed that the walls remained straight and vertical. The problem was the paint – it was sagging badly.

Let us revisit the layers. Upon the plaster was the original layer of whitewash – the same whitewash that developed rusty streaks. Over it was a layer of orange paint, and over that, the Tricolor layer, Union Jack layer, then yellow, green, and the final coat of violet. Six layers of paint clung to each other, all of them depended on the orange layer for adhesion. However, the orange layer was oil-based, and it never did attach well to the plaster. Under the weight of five more coats, it started to peel. And of course, everyone knew that once it had fallen off, the original blood-stained whitewash would be exposed once more…

The 'Bleeding Church'!

The Governor declared a State of Emergency. Scaffolds were set up and frantic efforts were made to thumb-tack the multiple layers back on the wall, but it proved futile. One Sunday, as the congregation gathered for the service, a huge patch on the upper left corner fell off entirely, revealing… a smooth, uniform surface, of a deep and lovely red.

What happened?

The original whitewash was mixed with water, and the dissolved iron was evenly spread; but oxidation depended on exposure to heat and rain, thus it occurred in uneven streaks and splotches.

The thick layers of paint added to the surface formed an airtight layer, but brick and plaster are porous, and over the centuries air percolated slowly into the wall *from behind.*

Rusting continued, slowly and out of sight, it went on, and on, until *all* the iron that could oxidise finally oxidised; and anything that could rust, rusted. Stains and splotches vanished as the entire surface turned red – a uniform, consistent and enchanting russet.

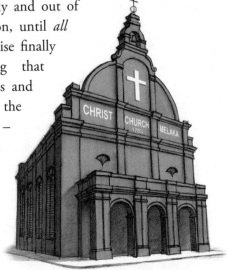

True color at last.

Happily, the Malaccans pulled off all the remaining swatches of paint. Like sunburnt skin peeling off to reveal fresh new skin below, the church emerged from centuries of paint to reveal its... *true colors.* All's well that ends well – and that is how it remains to this day.

AFTERWORD

Edward de Bono, author of *Lateral Thinking*, spent a holiday in Malacca and found out the truth. In his follow-up book, *Diagonal Thinking*, he wrote delightedly: "Ignore the problem, maybe it will go away."

26 SHAMELESS HUSSY!

To the world, the Eiffel Tower represents Paris and perhaps France itself; therefore, it may come as a shock that there was a time when not everyone thought so. When the French government decided to keep the Tower after the closing of the 1889 Paris Exposition (for which it had been built), there were many Parisians who bitterly objected to 'the iron giraffe' which they felt ruined the skyline of their beloved city. But no foes were as bitter as Bishop Dubuffet of Pissoir-en-Mise, although his objections were – surprisingly – on moral rather than aesthetic grounds.

"There she stands," the Bishop thundered. "This shameless iron hussy with her legs wide open, in a pose that would make a whore of Babylon blush!" He spearheaded a small but vocal campaign, consisting mainly of housewives from the Toulouse region, to 'tame this shameless slut of steel'. Eventually, in January 1895, a petition was sent to the Chamber of Deputies.

It seemed amazing that the Deputies did not throw the petition out on the spot. However, this occurred during the Dreyfus Affair (a Jewish army officer unfairly convicted of treason), a bitter controversy that split French society from top to bottom, and the Chamber of Deputies was similarly riven… and distracted.

Alfred Des Moules, a Deputy, recalled afterwards: "We could hardly hear anything, for in the left corner two Deputies were screaming at each other about the Dreyfus case. To the right, Monsieur Retarde had just called Monsieur Lapompe 'a dirty Jew' and they were strangling one another. The Speaker was desperately shouting over the uproar. I heard something about '… Eiffel Tower… filthy… shameful… clean up…'. It was true that the Champ de Mars had been getting rather rubbishy as of late. I assumed the bill was to clean up the vicinity, so I voted for it, all the time wondering why this little matter had come to the Chamber, instead of being attended to by the mayor."

The only surviving photograph of the 'decent' Eiffel Tower.

Armed with the bill, the Bishop hurried to sculptor Auguste Rodin, who was out of work ever since the *Burghers of Calais*. Rodin set to work at once, and a week later his masterpieces were sent to the Eiffel Tower and installed. The next morning, *tout Paris* awoke to see the Eiffel Tower 'decently' clad with four gigantic bronze fig leaves, decorously hiding the 'crotch' of each arch.

After a stunned silence, the deluge. The Chamber was excoriated for permitting this to happen, and Rodin was stoned in the streets. Abuse was showered on the Bishop and his band of 'tiny-minded prudes from Toulouse'. In retaliation, the defiant Bishop organised a march of his housewives, ending underneath the Tower, where he read aloud a congratulatory telegram from ex-Empress Eugenie de Montijo: "I had always felt uneasy about the Tower, that something wasn't quite correct. You have shown us what was wrong, and restored respectability to our great nation!"

Le Figaro detected a British plot to 'impose English hypocrisy and take away the liberties of France'. This predictably drew an icy retort from British Prime Minister William Gladstone: "The French are perfectly capable of being asses on their own, without any help from us."

Gustav Eiffel, the designer of the Tower, sent a telegram to Rodin: "I forgive you, for I know you must eat, and I hope you choke." On the other hand, Rodin was deeply embittered. "Why is it that nobody even noticed that all four leaves are *different?* After all my trouble! Parisians are such philistines!"

But there were some who kept their perspectives – and humour. Actress Sarah Bernhardt threw a party; her guests arrived to find all the legs of the dining chairs covered by ladies' underwear. (One wonders where she found four-legged versions.) Playwright Oscar Wilde also waded into the fray: "I had always thought the French were every bit as clever as the English. Now I know they are every bit as stupid."

But probably the best *bon mot* was uttered by writer Emile Zola, who took time off from the Dreyfus case to exclaim, "*Eh bien*, but what about her *breasts*?"

In the end, the storms of men were no match for those of nature. Two weeks later, a ferocious Atlantic storm blew in, and for twenty-four hours Paris was assaulted by gales. The fig leaves, which were never securely bolted down, got shredded and fragments blew all over the city, most of them landing within the compound of the nearby Ecole Militaire. The cadets, gleefully invoking an ancient (and possibly non-existent) law of salvage, collected and sold the fragments to a scrap dealer. With the proceeds they held a fête, during which many toasts were drunk to the health of the Bishop, praising him as '*Le homme honnête et respectable*'. We can be sure the toasts were tongue-in-cheek, since the party was held at the notorious Moulin Rouge, which the cadets had booked for the entire night. Painter Henri de Toulouse-Lautrec, who popped in for a peek, wrote: "I saw La Goulue doing things with her anatomy that I would not have believed possible."

Rodin survived the storm. Years later, he was commissioned by *Le Société des Gens des Lettres* to produce a statue of the writer Honore Balzac. He struggled with the commission, showing Balzac as a heroic naked man – which was taking considerable liberty with the truth, as the real Balzac was a

Balzac without fig leaf.

big fat slob. However, *that* was not the problem when a member from the *Société* came to see the clay model.

"The fig leaf, Monsieur! The fig leaf!" the man hissed, glaring at the naked Balzac. Rodin hurriedly wrapped Balzac in shapeless lumpy draperies, and today it is considered one of his finest works.

27 SINFUL SINGAPORE

Telok Ayer Market… a dull, respectable market in dull, respectable Singapore.
- It was a Victorian-era building. *(Yawn.)*
- It is a National Monument. *(Snore.)*

And yet, who could guess that this dull, respectable old market was once…
- The most wanton place in Asia?
- The Babylon of the East?
- The Fleshpot of the Orient?
- *Sinful Singapore!*

Telok Ayer Market — boring, boring, boring…

In 1890, the colonial government of Singapore, having reclaimed the shallow water off Telok Ayer, reserved a square plot of land between Robinson Road and Raffles Quay for a new market. However, strapped for cash, they decided not to build the market, but held a public tender – the winner would build and operate the market for ninety-nine years, after which it would revert to the British government.

"A public tender, what?" muttered Sir Charles Mitchell, Governor of the Straits Settlement. "What is so tender about *our* public? A scruffy lot of Chinese, Malays, Indians – and Heavens-know-who. *I* haven't seen anything tender since arriving in Singapore!"

"A tender means a *bid*, Sir Charles," James MacRitchie, the Municipal Engineer, murmured. "You know, like an auction."

"And who won, pray?" Sir Charles demanded.

MacRitchie opened an envelope. "A French consortium… called *'Le Publique'*… I say! Their director is named Auguste Le Rogue! What a name!"

"Never trust a rogue," Sir Charles snarled. "Never trust the French."

Auguste Le Rogue turned out to be a dapper little Frenchman, with a thin moustache. "Ah! *Mon nom!* It is comical, no? Alas, I am stuck with it. Look you, I am from Normandy, and my ancestor was a Viking. His name was Eric the Red." He pronounced it "Ehr-REEK". "So, our family name is *Le Rouge*. It means red!"

"Then how did you turn into a *Rogue*?" MacRitchie asked.

"The clerk who registered our name was an imbecile. He

reversed the 'u' and 'g'. But, enough of my silly name. The paper is ready, shall we sign?"

Le Rogue produced the contract, decorated with seals and ribbons, and handed it to Ahmed, Sir Charles' clerk. Ahmed laid it on the table. Le Rogue and Sir Charles signed, shook hands and the deal was done.

Never trust a rogue.

The market, designed by MacRitchie, was an octagonal 'wheel' that fitted neatly into the square plot of land, with eight 'spokes' that met in the centre, over which was a little clock tower. The gaps between the spokes were open to the sky, providing light and ventilation.

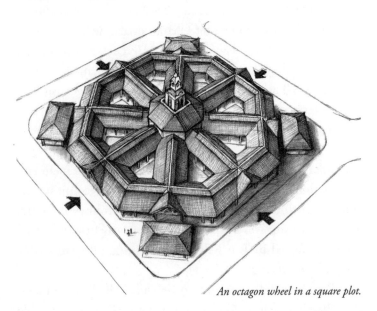

An octagon wheel in a square plot.

Le Rogue inspected the plans. "Why these columns, they are so thick?"

"They are brick columns, Sir. And I cannot make them thinner, for they may buckle."

"Ah! I understand. But I want them thinner. Why not iron? Yes! Slender iron columns, supporting arches above, and with frilly lacy filigree!" Le Rogue doodled a sketch, with lots of curlicues.

"But Monsieur, cast iron is expensive!" Sir Charles pointed out. He peered at Le Rogue's little doodle. "And, your curly decoration will cost even more!"

"Ah… What is money, compared to beauty?" sighed the Frenchman. "As your Shakespeare said, 'a thing of beauty is a joy forever' – yes?"

"I think it was Keats who said it," MacRitchie scratched his head.

"Me, I prefer Kipling," Sir Charles muttered.

"How do you *kipple*?" Le Rogue asked, mischievously.

Sir Charles groaned. "Monsieur, *that* joke has whiskers on it."

"Never mind, never mind," Le Rogue chortled, pushing his sketch over to MacRitchie.

"Well Sir, it's *your* money," MacRitchie peered at the doodle and shrugged. "Ours not to reason why, ours but to doodle and die."

The iron columns and arches – with 'frilly lacy filigree' – was cast in Glasgow and sent to Singapore, where a local contractor, Chea Keow, erected it. The roof was added, the clock tower erected, and…

"I want to add a few more things…" Le Rogue said, unrolling a plan.

Chea Keow gazed at the drawing, puzzled. "Alamak! What for you want this?"

The additional items were: a raised platform in the 'hub', various counters within the eight 'spokes' and the octagonal 'wheel' was to be subdivided into individual cubicles, with walls nine feet high.

"This one a market lah, what for you want walls so high?" demanded Chea Keow.

"Never mind, just build it," Le Rogue whispered. "Don't tell the Brits."

Sir Charles was invited to the Grand Opening. "What? *At seven in the evening?*" he exclaimed. "An odd time to open a market, what!"

"I say, the French are damn odd!" MacRitchie muttered.

Even odder still, as they approached the market, they saw it lit up from top to bottom with bright gas-lights. Thumping loud music emerged, punctuated with female voices screaming.

"I say!" MacRitchie exclaimed. "Jolly noisy for a market, what?"

At the main entrance, Ahmed and Chea Keow were waiting – looking dazed. Le Rogue emerged and opened his arms. "Welcome! Welcome to my *Market of Dreams!*" he exclaimed, and gleefully brought everyone into…

SINFUL SINGAPORE!

Le Rogue had organised the place as efficiently as a meat factory. The arriving visitor was 'processed' in four consecutive zones:

Zone 1: from any of the four main entrances, the visitor entered a main 'spoke' – filled with bar counters and stools, selling everything from beer to *mao-tai*. This was to soften up the clientele. The visitor – suitably inebriated – was then irresistibly attracted to…

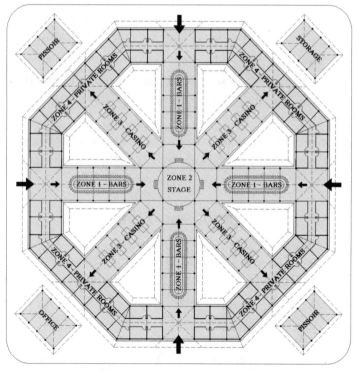

MacRitchie's plan, revised by Auguste Le Rogue.

Zone 2: the bright and noisy hub, where a troupe of Cantonese can-can dancers were kicking up their heels on a raised stage, pulling up their skirts as they delivered high kicks. Slippers flew in all directions as they screamed, "Sin-Sin-Singapore!" As the horrified Brits watched, they were replaced by Eskimo belly-dancers. Mingling with the audience were various 'Belles Orientale' who gleefully accosted any males within reach, crying, "Hell-oooo!" and "Remember me?" The visitor, befuddled, was then dragged off to…

Zone 3: the four minor 'spokes', filled with gambling tables. Nearby were couches fitted with *hookahs*, but they smelled not of tobacco but sickly sweet, like opium. After the visitor had gambled (or smoked) away most of his cash, his 'Belle Orientale' would usher him – now completely addled – to…

Zone 4: these were the cubicles in the 'rim' of the wheel. Now it was clear why the walls were so high – what happened inside was definitely *not* for public view.

SINFUL SINGAPORE!

Be it noted that, although there were four grand entrances, there were no designated exits. The visitor was left to stumble his way out, as best as he could…

Sir Charles gasped as the Eskimo belly-dancers were replaced by geishas on flying trapeze. "What have you done?" he screamed at Le Rogue. "You call this a market? *It's a bordello!*"

Le Rogue shrugged. "*Alors*, you Brits are so pedestrian. To you a market means only pots and pans! This, Monsieur, is a *Market of Dreams. A Bazaar of the Senses!*"

"More like a meat market," MacRitchie muttered, as he eyed the 'Belles Orientale' warily. "What you are selling are ladies of the night!"

"Not exactly *ladies,*" Ahmed said. He glanced at a few flat-chested, narrow-hipped specimens. "I'm not sure if some of them are *women,*" he added.

"I say – a bazaar of the bizarre, what?" MacRitchie rolled his eyes upwards.

Le Rogue followed his gaze, "Ah, Monsieur, now you understand why I wanted those arches filled with frilly filigree!" He lowered his voice to a conspiratorial whisper. "They are suggestive, no? Like a woman's lacy undergarment! *A woman's secret weapon!*"

"You mean these filigrees are supposed to suggest... a woman's *panties?*" Sir Charles cried.

"Well, I say!" MacRitchie, shocked.

Le Rogue grinned, "What man can resist? Panties to make him pant!" He winked at Sir Charles, "I bet that's the secret weapon your Queen Victoria used to ensnare Prince Albert... it is Victoria's secret!"

"Are you implying our Queen bared her... her..." Sir Charles stammered, turning crimson.

Lacy underwear up high.

"Well, it could hardly be her *face,*" Le Rogue shrugged.

The next night, Sir Charles sent in the police. They found the market surrounded by scattered food vendors. Hawkers followed the crowd. Food stalls sprouted overnight, like mushrooms. The policemen walked past rickety tables and stools, and at a signal, raided *Sinful Singapore.* But before they could blow their whistles, the 'Belles Orientale' jumped – three or four ladies to one man, hugging, kissing and stroking. Under this onslaught the policemen flailed about and toppled to the floor, with the ladies still clinging on, like leeches.

Policemen in those days wore khaki shorts – very wide and jutted out sideways, like those in Lat's cartoons. It was easy for the 'Belles Orientale' to slip their hands up the men's thighs and…

"What happened?" Sir Charles scowled as the policemen limped out of the market, covered in smeared lipstick, rouge and mascara, their caps askew.

"Sir, they raped us!" they wailed.

The Public Prosecutor charged Auguste Le Rogue with 'encouraging lewd and indecent behaviour'.

"Please, what is meaning of lewd?" Le Rogue asked, innocently. "My English not so good."

"It means indecent," the Public Persecutor sternly informed him.

"So! What is meaning of indecent?"

"It means lewd…" the Public Prosecutor stammered,

having defined himself into a circle. "It means exposing a part of the... um... anatomy... that... uh... is forbidden..."

"Such as?" Le Rogue asked.

"Such as... the *chest*..."

Le Rogue looked puzzled. "Men have chests. What do women have?"

But of course, the icily prudish Victorian could not reply. He simply could *not* bring himself to utter the words 'breasts' or 'thighs' – let alone (Heavens forbid!) 'nipples'. He stared helplessly, tongue-tied and face turning crimson.

"Ta-ta, gentlemen," Le Rogue waved as he traipsed out of the court. "It seems like *your* English not so good either. Call me when you can speak. *Adieu*."

Sir Charles arrested Le Rogue for trafficking in opium.

"What's wrong with opium?" Le Rogue asked, indignantly. "You sell tons of it to the Chinese."

"Well... that's for *export*," Sir Charles stuttered. "It is forbidden for the English!"

"Ah well, I will tell them not to sell to any Englishman. *Oui?*"

"I would not even feed it to a dog!" cried Sir Charles, losing his cool.

"Very well, I take note," Le Rogue said, coldly.

The next day a sign appeared above the opium den: 'ENGLISHMEN AND DOGS NOT ALLOWED'

Back at City Hall, Sir Charles wailed, "What shall we *do?*"

"Well, I say!" muttered MacRitchie.

"They even got *ah-gua* in there," Ahmed added.

"They got *what?*" Sir Charles asked, glaring at his clerk.

Ahmed turned pink and said, "Uh… '*ah-gua*' is local slang, Sir… It means a man who dresses like a woman."

"Transvestites!" MacRitchie hissed. "Well, I say! That's too much!"

"James, stop *say*-ing and *do* something!" Sir Charles bellowed!

"What?"

"Arrest them! 'Unnatural sex' or 'behaviour contrary to nature'… whatever!"

Once again, the police raided *Sinful Singapore*, clad in thick woollen trousers. By now the streets around the market were filled with hawkers, displaying rows of roast ducks and tanks of live lobsters.

"Well, I say!" MacRitchie growled. "What a lot of pests, what?"

"We'll deal with them later," Sir Charles grunted. "Once this place is closed, they'll disperse anyway!"

The 'women' were arrested, not without a struggle. Some took off their high-heels and whacked the policemen on the heads. They were all dragged off to gaol, screaming and struggling.

Once again, Auguste Le Rogue came to court.

"I must complain of this treatment!" he cried. "Police brutality!"

"We are acting within British law," Sir Charles said severely.

"Then, call it *Brit*ality!" Le Rogue sneered. "Look you, some of the women were badly hurt!"

"They are *not* women," Sir Charles snarled.

"They *are* women."

"They are *men*!"

"Prove it," Le Rogue retorted.

But of course, they couldn't. Stripping the 'women' would be 'lewd and indecent behaviour'.

"They are *ah-gua*!" Sir Charles cried. "Even the locals can tell! They are transvestites!"

"You heard wrong, Monsieur," Le Rogue replied coldly. "The correct word is *Aqua*. It is Latin for 'water' because these ladies are as beautiful as water!"

The 'Aqua' started to sing in Mandarin: "*The Maidens of Alishan are as beautiful as water…*"

They pranced about and kissed each other.

"Unnatural sex!" cried Sir Charles triumphantly. "Sodomy!"

Le Rogue rose wearily. "Monsieur, I have tolerated your interference enough!" he cried. He pulled out a document and plonked it before Sir Charles. It was the contract, awarding the market to Le Rogue's consortium. "If you be so kind as to read the words?" Le Rogue said, pointing.

Sir Charles peered – and suddenly froze.

What the wording should have said was: "*… the property shall be ceded to Le Publique, of France, for a duration of ninety-nine years…*" But through some incredible slip of the pen, what it *actually* said was: "*… the property shall be ceded to The Republic of France for a duration of ninety-nine years…*"

In short, the British had ceded the market to another nation.

"Well, I say!" MacRitchie started, but choked as Sir Charles throttled him.

"And *here* in France," Le Rogue said serenely, "We follow

Poster by Toulouse-Lautrec.

the *Napoleonic Code.* Sodomy is not a crime. *Ta-ta.*"

He walked out, majestically, leaving both Brits open-mouthed and staring at one another.

Never, ever trust a rogue.

The news that a chunk of Singapore had been ceded to France caused outrage around the British Empire (and considerable glee elsewhere). Parliament screamed. Sir Charles was ordered to take back the territory, by force if necessary. Her Majesty was *not* amused by 'Victoria's Secret'.

The battleship *Insufferable* arrived, carrying battle-hardened soldiers fresh from the Boer War. Reinforced by the Singapore Volunteer Rifles Corps, they attacked. The soldiers kicked aside tables, stools and woks, sending the vendors fleeing. The artillery aimed their cannons at the clock tower whilst riflemen surrounded the market, and with a bugle call, they charged...

... and found the place empty.

The stage was silent, the bar counters deserted. A few 'Belles Orientale' sat around gloomily. When they saw the soldiers, they yelled: "You got money, big boys? We hadn't been paid for months!"

Puzzled, Sir Charles and MacRitchie broke into Le Rogue's office. It, too, was deserted. Le Rogue had fled. A quick examination of the files revealed an incredible answer:

Sinful Singapore was… bankrupt!

The consortium had borrowed heavily and was up to its eyebrows in debt. Construction was costly (what with those 'frilly filigrees') and the Eskimo belly-dancers did not come cheap. Yet, how *could* it fail? Given the carnal delights it offered, it *should* have been raking in money by the barrow-loads.

The Forbidden Fruit fell to the ground – and nobody even nibbled. The Whore of Babylon opened her legs – and everybody just yawned.

The sad truth was this: although night after night the place was filled with local yokels, *hardly anybody bought anything.* They drank a few beers, gawped at the dancers, spent a few dollars on the roulette and then marched out to…

The hawkers.

Mouth-watering satays – dripping with rich sauce! Piping hot rotis, crispy at the edges! Crimson chilli-crabs, hot enough to blow off the roof of your mouth!

With food like these, who *wants* to sin?

The army cleared away the stage and counters and tore down the nine-foot partitions. Then, MacRitchie divided up the space and moved the hawkers inside. At least it cleared the streets for traffic once again.

As the last of the hawkers moved his tables and stools into the market, Ahmed remarked to Chea Keow, "We Singaporeans *lah*… we don't know *how* to sin."

"Yeah," Chea Keow shrugged. "We just eat."

28 AMERICAN ICON

The word 'icon' is badly abused. Originally it meant a sacred image, but nowadays it means anything famous, or something you click on with your mouse. But in one case, the term is well deserved.

The four colossal faces on Mount Rushmore were carved by sculptor Gutzon Borglum from 1927 to 1941. Since completion they had been visited by millions of camera-toting admirers, becoming a national 'icon' in the full sense of the word, for it portrays – *The Great Gods of America.*

Yup, you heard me. They are *GODS.* At least that was the view of a crazy old carpenter from Guangzhou…

Larry Yung was not an 'ABC' (American-Born Chinese) but came close to it. Born in 1920 to a poor carpenter outside Guangzhou, he was sent by his father to San Francisco in 1935 (after his mother died) to join his uncle, who owned a small laundry shop in Chinatown. By working hard and studying harder, Larry obtained an Engineering degree and settled into a comfortable job in Palo Alto, near San Francisco.

The Great Gods of America.

In the early fifties, worried about his father being stuck in China, he managed to pull enough strings to get him out of the commune and onward to Hong Kong, and eventually to San Francisco – a bewildered old man with a battered suitcase, clutching a small ivory Guanyin.

"Baba, welcome to America!" said Larry grandly, to his father.

To Larry's surprise, Baba (father) took in his stride Larry's wife Caterina, who came from the Caribbean, and his best friend Steven, who was a negro. (Dear Reader: don't write angry letters. 'Negro' was a polite term back then – read Martin Luther King's speeches.) Baba was amused by drive-in theatres and bemused by drive-in hamburgers, but it was when Larry took him to Mount Rushmore that he had his epiphany.

They had just gotten out of the car when Baba gazed up at the four giant faces, froze, fell on his knees and started to kow-tow.

"What are you doing?" Larry cried.

"Get down!" Baba hissed. "Have you no respect for the gods?"

Larry rolled his eyes. "Baba, those aren't gods. They are men."

"Nonsense! Obviously, they are gods. How else can they be carved so big?"

As Baba came from a country where giant Buddhas were carved out of mountain cliffs, it seemed perfectly natural to him that the four giant faces were gods of some sort.

"Baba, get up – everybody's staring," Larry hissed, red-face. "They are not gods, they are *presidents.*"

"What is 'president'?"

"They govern the country, Baba."

"See! They are emperors! And emperors must be venerated!" And he kow-towed again.

"Baba! They are not emperors, just ordinary men who got elected."

"That's because they have the Mandate of Heaven!" Baba replied, with maddening logic.

Larry managed to pry his embarrassing father loose. They drove all the way back to Palo Alto in silence. A week later, Baba vanished.

Larry nearly went mad, contacting the police and calling up everyone he knew in Chinatown, but in the end, it was the park management at Mount Rushmore that found the old man.

Incredibly, this old man – with rudimentary English and no geography – had somehow found his way to Mount Rushmore, inveigled his way in, and collected enough wood and zinc sheets to build a tiny shack on a slope facing the four faces. By the time the park management noticed, he was erecting an altar.

He was jettisoned, of course. Larry persuaded the authorities not to put his father in a lunatic asylum. "He's not crazy," he told them. "Just nuts, that's all."

Back in Palo Alto, after a long lecture from his son, Baba seemed to settle in. No more mention was made of Mount Rushmore. Steven taught Baba English. Caterina taught him some Spanish. The old man learnt the bus routes to Chinatown and made friends. He bought a book, *The Presidents of the United States*, written in Chinese. In retrospect, Larry should have recognised the warning signs. But sons are always oblivious…

Six months later, Baba said he was spending a month of 'Vegetarian Retreat' at a temple.

"I'll drive you there!" Larry said, glad that his father found an interest.

"Oh no… You are busy with your projects. I'll go on my own. I know the buses already."

A month later, Larry drove to the temple to pick up his father. He was aghast to find that his father never showed up. But this time round, Larry had a pretty shrewd idea where to find his dad…

Sure enough, Baba was at Mount Rushmore. He had bought a tiny plot of land near Keystone, a little settlement to the east of the monument. The land had a view of Mount Rushmore – not a good view, being far away and at an awkward angle – but a view, nonetheless. To buy it, he had taken money from Larry's safe – but from his point of view, he wasn't stealing. And, he was building himself a shack.

"Baba, come home!" Larry wailed.

"Gods must be respected!" Baba replied, lugging a piece of wood.

"Baba, they aren't even Chinese gods!" Larry pointed out.

"So what? We are in America. We worship American gods."

It must be realised that the Chinese peasant's approach to religion is the same as his approach to food:

- If it looks edible, eat it.
- If it tastes bad, spit it out.
- If it looks like a god, worship it.
- If *that* tastes bad, spit it out.

Apparently, Washington and company were palatable.

Larry gave up. He hired a contractor to build his father a 'cabin' – he did not dare tell him the real purpose, but at least it would fulfil bylaws. Surprisingly, Baba and the contractor got along nicely, despite the language barrier.

"Your dad wants a picture window towards the Mount," he told Larry. "He likes the view."

"If you only knew," Larry muttered to himself, *sotto voce.*

When the cabin was ready, Baba moved in, and set up

an altar in front of the big picture window through which a distant view of the four faces was visible. To the side he added another altar, for his ivory Guanyin. Next to that, was a crucifix, given to him by Caterina. Each altar was provided with candles, incense, and offerings of fruits and sweets.

It may seem contradictory that a man can worship several gods at once. But the Chinese had always welcomed plenitude – the more the merrier. (They would have felt right at home in Ancient Greece and Rome.) In fact, they look upon monotheists with pity: "You only got *one* god? Oh, poor thing. He must be really overloaded! Here, try *this* god, very effective, you know…"

Caterina and Steven came to visit Larry and his dad. The following is a transcript of their conversation, with Larry translating.

"Baba, what god is this?" Caterina asked, pointing to George Washington.

"Ah, this is *Hua-sen-ten*," Baba replied, pronouncing the name in Chinese. "He is the God of War. He showed his martial quality even as a boy, when he cut down his father's cherry tree!"

"What has the cherry tree got to do with it?" Steven asked, puzzled.

"Wah! A little boy running around with an axe, chopping things down! So scary! No wonder when he got older, he chopped down *people*!"

The other three stared at him.

"He rode into battle, swinging his great axe, just like

Guangung!" Baba continued, with relish. "With one sweep he cut off a hundred English heads! That's why they are called 'Redcoats' – all splattered!"

Caterina whispered to Steven. "You know, there *is* a certain method in his madness."

"Or rather, madness in his methods," Steven whispered back.

Larry said, "Baba, they didn't use axes anymore. They had rifles."

"They used rifles?" Baba sounded disappointed. "Is that why you Americans are so fond of guns?" He opened a cupboard, revealing a shotgun.

"Baba, where did you get this?" Larry demanded, alarmed.

"Heh heh! I always wanted one," Baba chuckled, side-stepping the question.

Steven steered the conversation back to the 'gods', "Who is this one?" He pointed to Abraham Lincoln.

"That's *Ling-ken*, God of Liberty."

"And this one?" Caterina asked, pointing to Theodore Roosevelt.

"*Lo-si-fu*, God of Power. He is soft-spoken but beats everyone with a huge stick!" Baba got up and yawned. "It's time for my nap."

"Wait!" Steven said. "There's one more."

"That one?" Baba sounded reluctant. "That one is *Jia-fu-sen*, God of Hypocrites."

"*Hypocrites?*" everyone cried. "Jefferson?"

"He wrote something about every man being equal," Baba said.

"Declaration of Independence," Steven said to Larry. "I

think your dad knows more American history than *you* do!"

Ignoring Steven's jibe, Larry asked, "Why should that make him a hypocrite?"

"He owned slaves," Baba replied. "Lots of them."

Steven said, with heavy irony, "It's *not* hypocrisy. White people simply didn't consider us *humans*. We were *animals*, you know, like dogs and cats." There was considerable bitterness in his voice.

Baba replied, "But white people taught your people to worship Jesus."

Caterina mused, "I see your point. If you can worship God, and know good from evil, then – by any reasonable definition, you're not an animal, but human!"

"I read that Jefferson once beat a slave for stealing food. Would he beat his dog?" Larry remarked.

"Of course not," Caterina said. "Animals don't know ethics. They just eat, and you can only blame your own carelessness. But if a *slave* ate his master's dinner – he gets beaten into a pulp!"

"In short, people like Jefferson enslaved us because we were 'animals' – yet expected us to behave like moral beings!" Steven cried. "Baba, you are right! It really *was* hypocrisy!"

"Wasn't there some rumour about him marrying a slave-woman?" Larry muttered.

"Not marriage," Steven said. "He had a long-term relationship with one of his slaves, Sally Hemings. She bore him children."

"All men enslave their wives, no matter their race," Caterina fumed.

"Honey, I *do* wash the dishes," Larry muttered in a small voice.

"Did he free her?" Baba asked, curious.

"No," Steven said.

"See! What a hypocrite!" Caterina cried triumphantly.

"But how can a hypocrite like him get to be a god?" Steven asked, indignantly.

Baba thought a bit before replying. "Everybody needs a god," he said, pragmatically. "And since the world is full of hypocrites, they need a god too, right?"

"Isn't it ironic, to put a slave-owner together with a slave-liberator?" Caterina said.

Baba laughed. "That is why *Ling-ken* pushed himself to the far right. He doesn't want to be *caught dead* next to this *Jia-fu-sen*."

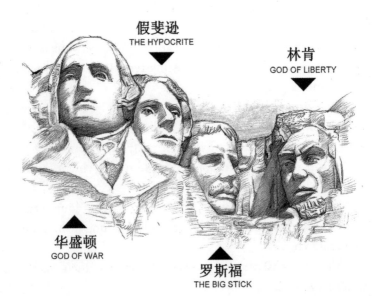

"You know, Lincoln *is* out of sequence," Steven remarked. "By historical chronology, he should have been placed *between* Jefferson and Roosevelt – not at the far right."

"Exactly. He couldn't *stand* that Big Hypocrite," Baba yawned. "Now I need my nap."

As news spread, the people of Keystone got uneasy. Some came to protest and were met by Larry.

"Freedom of Worship," he grunted. "Read the Constitution."

"But they are presidents, not gods!"

"To my dad they are gods, so who are you to say no?"

A Catholic priest came to object – he was met by Caterina.

"There is only one God," he said firmly. "How can there be four?"

"Why Father," Caterina said sweetly. "If I remember my catechism, there's the Trinity. If there's three, why not four?"

"The Holy Trinity had been united! They are one!"

"Ooh! So, you are a Unitarian! Does your Bishop know?"

The priest gave her a dirty look and departed.

A Lutheran pastor came to protest – he was met by Steven.

"The presidents were men, not gods."

"So was Jesus," Steven replied, sweetly.

"Jesus was man *and* God! He performed miracles, like turning water into wine."

"Lincoln turned slaves into citizens. Wasn't that an even bigger miracle?"

The pastor gave him a dirty look and departed.

Words spread. The little temple was featured in newspapers and magazines. Television film crews showed up. Some Americans were outraged, some were embarrassed; but most were bemused.

The Sons of the American Revolution organised a protest march to the little temple but were met by a furious scolding from Baba. "You call yourselves their *sons*? Where's your filial piety? *You* should be the one building this temple, not me! *You* should be the ones honouring your ancestors!" The SAR slunk away in embarrassment.

The National Rifle Association organised a demonstration. Baba, sick of being interrupted, fired warning shots at them with his shotgun. They made him a member on the spot.

Senator McCarthy smelled a Communist plot. He ordered an investigation, but the sub-committee drew a blank. Sure, it was un-American, but was Baba a *communist?* Karl Marx was an atheist. How can a godless communist worship a god – let alone *four* of them?

McCarthy was not satisfied and demanded an arrest, but lawyer Joseph Welsh exclaimed, "Have you no sense of decency, Sir, harrying a harmless old man? At long last, have you left no sense of decency?"

McCarthy fell from power and was burnt at the stake. (Actually, he wasn't, but should have been.)

The fusty fifties died, and the sixties roared in, swinging. It was the Age of Aquarius, the Summer of Love, hippies, LSD... Baba's little temple became the darling of the Counter-Culture. What could be more 'Counter' than inverting 'Culture'?

Hippies trickled in. Janis Joplin crooned 'Summertime' on the lawn. Andy Warhol pronounced, "In the future, everybody will be *divine* for fifteen minutes." The Beatles even planned an album with Mount Rushmore on the cover – their own faces replacing the four 'gods'. They gave up when they couldn't think of anything to rhyme with 'hypocrite'.

The devotees of Hare Krishna made a visit. Baba happily accepted their statue of Lord Krishna and added an altar, complete with garlands. By now the interior of the cabin was getting crowded. In addition to Guanyin, there were the three Buddhas, the Heavenly Queen (*not* to be confused with Guanyin), Jade Emperor (*not* married to the Heavenly Queen), Jesus and Virgin Mary (*not* to be confused with Guanyin), Brahma, Shiva, Vishnu, Rama, Parvathi and Ganesh... the more the merrier. In fact, it got so crowded that the Eight Immortals had to be perched on the roof.

"They are immortals," Baba said. "They can take a little rain."

Larry took his father to New York, where Baba knelt reverently before the Statue of Liberty. He bought the biggest replica in the souvenir shop and carried it back to Rushmore. After some thought he placed it on the extreme right end of the main altar, so it would appear next to Lincoln, the God of Liberty.

"Same surname," he mused. "They must be brother and sister."

Caterina heard him and said, "Just like Apollo and Artemis."

"No!" Larry cried, alarmed – but it was too late.

Baba turned and asked, "Who?"

As Larry refused to elucidate, Baba dived back into Chinatown and returned with a battered old copy of Thomas Bullfinches' *The Mythologies of Ancient Greece and Rome.*

"What have you *done*?" Larry whispered fiercely to his wife. "Where the hell are we going to find statues of Jupiter, Apollo, Athena and all the rest?"

But surprisingly, the old man did not demand new statues. Perhaps he had enough already; or perhaps because he also found a copy of an *Introduction to Greek Philosophy.*

And *that* would have even more surprising consequences...

All things must end. By the mid-seventies, the temple faded from public mind; fewer visitors came. Baba got older. In 1972, he died.

Larry moved all the bric-a-brac back to Palo Alto, then sold the land to a nearby supermarket, who demolished the temple to expand its carpark. Was Larry being unfilial, destroying his father's lifework? Actually, it was in accordance with the old man's last wishes.

When Baba collapsed, he was rushed to hospital and put in ICU, but everyone knew the end was near. After all, he was 90. Larry sat by the bed, along with Caterina and Steven, both of whom have become very attached to this crazy old man, infuriating and endearing.

Baba opened his eyes. "After I go, sell the land," he said weakly.

Larry was stunned. "What about your temple?"

"It doesn't matter," Baba said, pointing to a book. "There is this Greek guy who said, 'We all come from the Light. The soul can remember, or forget'."

"It sounds like Plato," Steven whispered, incredulously. "Or, Socrates."

"In some people, the Light shines bright," Baba said. "We set up altars and worship them as gods. But now I understand, what we actually worship is their Light."

"What Light?" Caterina asked.

"You know it. Everybody has it. It's that *thing* that scolds you when you did something bad and cheer you when you did something good. Even bad people have it – but they ignore it," he paused, and added. "So, you see, it doesn't really matter *which* god you worship."

Everybody was stunned. Larry asked, "Are you saying the gods don't really exist?"

"They exist," Baba replied, in a faraway voice. "So long as you worship them."

"Then why should we worship them?" Steven asked.

"Because they are the part of you worth worshipping."

Silence fell.

Then, Steven asked, "What about the Hypocrite god, *Jia-fu-sen*? Does *he* have the Light too?"

The old man's eyes popped open. "I think he was included by mistake! You know what smooth tongues hypocrites have. I bet he sweet-talked his way in! Why don't you buy some dynamite and blow his nose off?"

He guffawed; and died.

MEA CULPA

Dear Reader,

By the time you reach this, you must have realised (unless you have the intelligence of a termite) that everything in this book is just a load of bull. I only hope you had as much fun reading it as I had in cooking it up.

You are welcome to share these tall tales with your friends, but please do *not* send them snippets extracted from the book, nor post bits and pieces on social media. Little bits taken out of context may sound like serious information and cause genuine confusion. We have enough 'fake news' already – and I don't want some poor soul wasting his time searching the atlas for 'Guten-Baden' or 'Crumbledore-Upon-Scree', nor tramp the Great Wall looking for the Great Ditch…

Instead, send them a whole chapter or order them a copy of this book, thus giving them a decent chance to figure out that their legs are being pulled.

And if your friends *really* do believe it, then I seriously advise cutting off all contact with them. For clearly, *they* have the intelligence of termites.

ABOUT THE AUTHOR

Ho Kwoncjan was born in Bangkok, Thailand, whereupon his mother stabbed the letter "C" through his name, like a skewer, because she wanted the same initials as her father. This made his name unpronounceable, so he's widely and amiably called "KC".

Growing up in Bangkok, KC's first language was Cantonese, then Thai, then British-English, then American-English, then Mandarin (when his family moved to Singapore) and finally Singlish (when he was dragged into the Army). By the time he staggered into the National University of Singapore, he had become so linguistically traumatised he chose architecture, because "architects don't have to talk; they just grunt".

Upon graduation, the Singapore Institute of Architects gave him a Gold Medal, possibly for Creative Grunting, and maybe to get rid of him.

He divides his time between Singapore, where "the situation is serious, but not hopeless" and Bangkok, where it is "hopeless, but not serious". Whenever Singapore becomes too serious, he escapes to Bangkok, and when Bangkok floods, he returns.

In his occasional bouts of sanity, he designs hotels for the Banyan Tree Group. Some of them had won international design awards, but it is unclear what substances the judges had been abusing. His ambition is to build a whorehouse, but finding no client, he wrote this book instead. As they say, same-same.